Pre

VISUAL GRAMMAR

Picture it!

Practise it!

with answers

Jim Scrivener

 Richmond

Richmond

58 St Aldates
Oxford
OX1 1ST
United Kingdom

© 2014, Santillana Educación, S.L. / Richmond

Publisher: Deborah Tricker
Digital publisher: Luke Baxter
Content development: Anna Gunn
Editors: Eileen Flannigan, Zanna Taylor
Design and layout: Lorna Heaslip
Cover design: Mark Willey
Photo research: Magdalena Mayo
Art direction: Helen Reilly, Lorna Heaslip

With Key Edition ISBN: 978-84-668-1566-6

D.L. M-8268-2013

Printed in China

Publisher acknowledgements:
The Publisher would like to thank all those who have given their kind permission to reproduce material for this book:

Illustrations:
Phill Burrows, Ella Cohen, James Gilleard, Oscar, Dave Oakley, Reehan, Myles Talbot, Eva Thimgren

Photographs:
A. Real; G. Rodríguez; J. Jaime; J. Lucas; J. M.ª Escudero; S. Padura; A. G. E. FOTOSTOCK; ALAMY; COMSTOCK; CORBIS LONDRES; DIGITAL BANK; GETTY IMAGES SALES SPAIN/ Photos.com Plus, Thinkstock; HIGHRES PRESS STOCK/ AbleStock.com; ISTOCKPHOTO/Getty Images Sales Spain; NASA; REX FEATURES; SERIDEC PHOTOIMAGENES CD; ARCHIVO SANTILLANA

Every effort has been made to trace the holders of copyright before publication. The Publisher will be pleased to rectify any errors or omissions at the earliest opportunity.

Contents

Contents

Contents

Contents

Hello! My name's Jim and I'm a language teacher. My students find grammar difficult ... and *I* find grammar difficult when I'm learning other languages. So, I wanted to write a grammar book that could help you understand grammar better and make your study a little bit easier.

Learning English

If you want to learn English well, you need lots of **language**.

You need **words**.

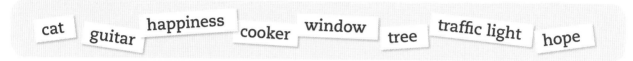

cat | guitar | happiness | cooker | window | tree | traffic light | hope

You need **collocations** and **chunks** – patterns of words that often go together.

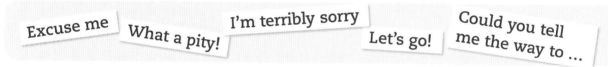

blonde hair | fast food | have a bath | a cup of coffee | pass an exam | give up

You need to know **common expressions** and **when to use them**.

Excuse me | What a pity! | I'm terribly sorry | Let's go! | Could you tell me the way to ...

You need to know the **pronunciation** of all these things (not just on their own, but when they are spoken in sentences).

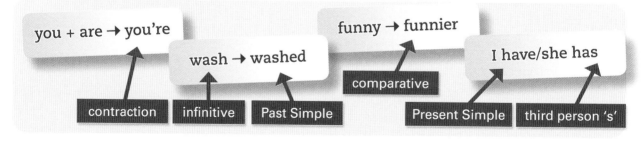

hill | heel | /fɪʃ ən ʧɪps/

And you need **grammar**.

you + are → you're · contraction | wash → washed · infinitive · Past Simple | funny → funnier · comparative | I have/she has · Present Simple · third person 's'

It's not important to know grammar names like these. But it IS important to understand how the grammar works.

Of course as well as this, you need lots and lots of **practice**.

Practice ... **Listening** to English. **Speaking** English. **Reading** it. **Writing** it. **USING** it!

You can communicate using just words without grammar – but your meaning will not be 100% clear.

Tony send Mary email.

It's like looking at a photograph that is out of focus or too dark. We have some idea of the meaning – but we aren't certain.

If we add grammar, we know much more, including:

time – when something happens

number – whether things are single or plural

actions – who does the action, how they do it and who they do it for or do it to

message – whether it's a statement, negative, question, request, order, etc.

Did Tony send Mary any emails?
Tony isn't going to send Mary that email.

Suddenly, our photo is clear and in focus.

This book will help you study grammar

Grammar is not just about studying patterns, word order and endings. You need to understand meanings and uses, too. This book will help you with all of these.

English grammar is sometimes very strange. For example, a tense called the Present Simple can be used to talk about past and future times, not only the present! In some grammar books you will find all these different meanings in one unit, or even on just one page. This can be very confusing for students. So, in this book, I give a whole unit for each meaning. You will understand the language more clearly and will have much more practice in using it.

Grammar practice doesn't have to be boring!

Do the exercises like games. Do them again and again. Write them. Speak them. Record yourself saying them. Listen to them on the bus or tram. Try and remember them while you are walking in town. Write text messages to your friends and use the language. Test each other. Cover the page and test yourself. Look at the pictures – can you remember what was on the page?

Most of all, enjoy it. See if you can find out why learning a language is exciting, interesting and fun.

Good luck!

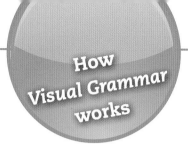

How Visual Grammar works

Pictures

The pictures help you understand the meaning of the language. They also help you remember the grammar.

Grammar boxes

The grammar boxes show you how to make the grammar. You will find the 'rules' of the language and examples.

Examples

There are lots of examples. They show you how the language is used. The examples show real English – as people speak it – not just 'Grammar book' language.

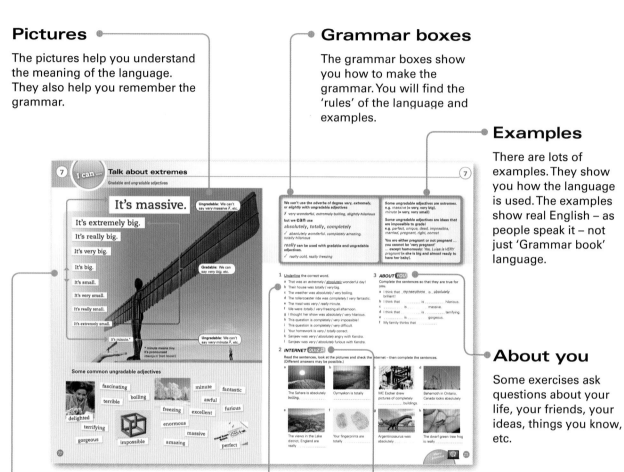

About you

Some exercises ask questions about your life, your friends, your ideas, things you know, etc.

Diagrams

The diagrams give you information about how the language works. For example, they show you that you must change the word order – or that you must change a word. Sometimes there are **timelines** that help you understand when something happens.

Exercises

The exercises give you lots of chances to practise using the language. Sometimes different answers are possible.

Internet quiz

In some exercises, you use the internet to find answers.

Word pool

Some exercises are word pools – a mixture of words. You must try to make sentences using the words. Many different answers are usually possible.

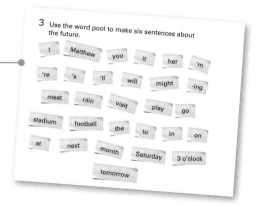

I can ... | Refer to people and things

Nouns, pronouns, pronoun reference

Nouns

helicopter is singular (i.e. one)

shoes are plural (i.e. more than one)

helicopter & *shoe* are countable nouns (*one shoe, two shoes, three shoes*, etc.)

water & *happiness* are uncountable nouns (✗ *one happiness, two happinesses*)

Jack is a 'proper name'. A proper name (e.g. the name of a person, an organisation, a town, a college, etc.) is written with a capital letter.

We can use a pronoun instead of a noun:

who **does** the action   who the action **happens to**

Subject	Object
I	me
you	you
he	him
she	her
it	it
we	us
they	them

Miranda was painting the boat.

She was painting it.

Jack gave the books to Sophie.

He gave them to her.

---

1 Answer the questions with words from the box. (You can use words more than once.)

> ~~Armenia~~   art   coin   furniture
> Harvard   magazine   money   music
> people   women

Find

a two proper names   *Armenia* ....

b two singular nouns   ....

c two plural nouns   ....

d four uncountable nouns   ....
                     ....

e four countable nouns   ....
                     ....

2 Complete the sentences. Use pronouns.

a I called at Mary's house, but __*she*__ wasn't in.

b This parcel is for Gareth and Wendy. Could you give it to .... , please?

c I think we're lost! I hope someone can tell .... the way to 16th Street.

d Oh no! Where's my wallet? I think I've left .... at home!

e Paul Gabriel? Paul Gabriel? I've heard that name before – but I don't think I've ever met ....

f I need the answer to question 7! Tell .... , please!

3 Look at the circled pronouns and <u>underline</u> the words that they refer to. Draw an arrow to connect them.

a <u>The old cinema</u> was in the centre of town. Astorico bought (it) last February.

b I've never seen a necklace like this before. (It's) so beautiful.

c The snow fell all night. When Marty woke up, (he) ran to the window and stared out in amazement. (It) was everywhere.

d I love the chocolate cakes that you can buy in this bakery. (They) are just so delicious!

e We asked for some help with the credit card problems at the reception desk, but the horrid man said (he) couldn't do anything to help (us) with (them).

f Keira and her friends got together and (they) decided to watch the *Wedding Disasters* DVD. But (it) didn't work.

Make sentences with good word order

Grammatical terms: subject, object, verb, SVO word order

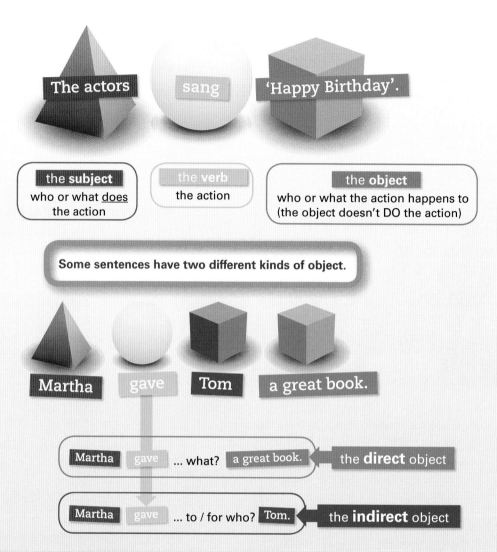

The actors | sang | 'Happy Birthday'.

the subject
who or what <u>does</u> the action

the verb
the action

the object
who or what the action happens to
(the object doesn't DO the action)

Some sentences have two different kinds of object.

Martha | gave | Tom | a great book.

Martha | gave | ... what? | a great book. ← the **direct** object

Martha | gave | ... to / for who? | Tom. ← the **indirect** object

The most common word order in English:

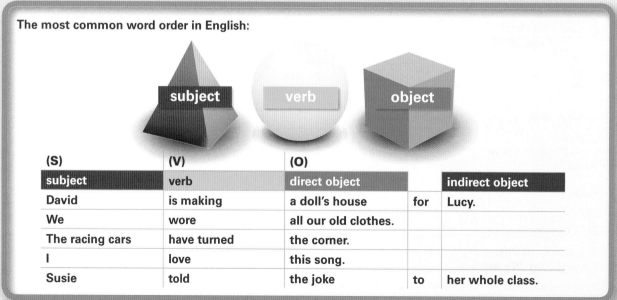

subject | **verb** | **object**

(S)	(V)	(O)		
subject	verb	direct object		indirect object
David	is making	a doll's house	for	Lucy.
We	wore	all our old clothes.		
The racing cars	have turned	the corner.		
I	love	this song.		
Susie	told	the joke	to	her whole class.

The indirect object can come before the direct object:

David is making Lucy a doll's house.

Susie told her whole class the joke.

How to recognise them?

the **direct** object	the **indirect** object
Ask 'what ...?' or 'who ...?'	Ask 'to who ...?' or 'for who ...?' or 'with who ...?' or 'what ...?'
e.g. *David is making what? Susie told who?*	e.g. *David is making the doll's house for who? Susie told the joke to who?*

Martin cooked a wonderful pizza for Liz. ✓
(subject – verb – object – object)

Martin cooked Liz a wonderful pizza. ✓
(subject – verb – object – object)

Martin a wonderful pizza cooked for Liz. ✗
(subject – object – verb – object)

Martin for Liz cooked a wonderful pizza. ✗
(subject – object – verb – object)

Martin for Liz a wonderful pizza cooked. ✗
(subject – object – object – verb)

We *give, say, sell, lend, write, send, show, teach* something **to** someone.

We *make, do, buy, get, cook, find* something **for** someone. We *ask* someone **for** something.

---

1 Circle the subject. Underline the direct object.

a Bill is visiting the art gallery.
b Sue made an Indian curry for George.
c I'll give the children five footballs.
d The teacher lent me his calculator.
e The whole class saw a fantastic film at the cinema.
f Wendy bought her daughter a new coat.
g Wendy bought a new coat for her daughter.

2 Put these pieces of sentences in the correct order – then label the pieces S (Subject), V (Verb), O (Object).

a for you | Karen | some new headphones | bought

Karen bought some new headphones for you.
 S   V   O   O

b I'm | my car | repairing

c is asking | the children | the teacher | for their homework

d me | sent | a letter | Terry

e a cold drink | will | get | us | Gill

f wrote | for me | Lenny | a short story

3 Complete the sentences with a direct object. (Many different answers are possible.)

a Harry was reading *a science book.*
b Sean sent his sister
c The chef made
d I decided to buy
e We asked our teacher

I can ... # Make simple descriptions

Adjectives

sound It's noisy!

purpose It's educational!

appearance It's beautiful!

age It's old!

taste It's salty!

shape It's round!

origin It's Greek!

colour It's purple!

opinion It's boring!

size It's huge!

temperature It's freezing!

Adjectives

We can use most adjectives in only two places:
before nouns:

It was a <u>slow</u> train.
They bought some <u>broken</u> pots.
He had an <u>expensive</u> watch.

after be and some other verbs (*become, seem, appear, look, sound, taste, feel*, etc.):

The train was <u>slow</u>.
The pots were <u>broken</u>.
It looked very <u>expensive</u>.

⚠ Some adjectives (*alive, asleep, alone, sorry, ill, ready, safe, sure*) are not usually used before nouns:

✓ *The monster was alive.*
✗ *It was an alive monster.*

⚠ Adjectives do not have a plural.

a purple **car**   purple **cars**

same form

Common adjective endings include: *-able*, *-al*, *-ful*, *-ic*, *-less*, *-ous/-ious*, and *-y*.

Many adjectives are formed from nouns.

noun	adjective	
beauty	beautiful	*The park's beautiful.*
friend	friendly	*She's very friendly.*
home	homeless	*Help the homeless.*
mystery	mysterious	*a mysterious noise*
nature	natural	*a natural smile*
photograph	photographic	*a photographic report*
poison	poisonous	*a poisonous snake*
wind	windy	*It was a windy day.*

Sometimes when an adjective is formed from a noun or a verb the spelling changes slightly. If you are not sure, use your dictionary to check.

Many adjectives are formed from verbs. Some are made from past participles (verb column 3).

verb	adjective	
burn	burnt	*The toast was burnt.*
break	broken	*I looked at the broken mirror.*

Some adjectives that are made from verbs have more than one form.

	freezing	*The weather was freezing.*
freeze	frozen	*We bought some frozen pizzas.*

Some adjectives are made with the ending *-able* or *-ive*.

enjoy	enjoyable	*an enjoyable afternoon*
attract	attractive	*an attractive swimming pool*

1 Write the adjectives made from the nouns. Some nouns can make more than one adjective.

a rain   *rainy* ....
b salt   ....
c week   ....
d religion ....
e sun   ....
f fame   ....
g danger ....
h noise   ....
i science ....
j wonder ....

2 Write the adjectives made from the verbs. Some verbs can make more than one adjective.

a taste   *tasty / tasteful* ....
b sleep   ....
c lose   ....
d shine   ....
e write   ....

3 Write the *-able* or *-ive* adjectives made from the verbs.

a enjoy   *enjoyable* ....
b act   ....
c create ....
d break   ....
e fashion ....
f kiss   ....
g attract ....

4 The adjectives in the sentences are mixed up. Correct them.

a She tried to open the door, but it was blonde.
   ....*locked*...................
b These chips are much too exhausted. ....
c The Sun was ~~locked~~. ....
d After seven hours of work, Miguel was slippery.
   ....
e That book about planets was very bright.
   ....
f He climbed over the wall. It was very educational.
   ....
g Has she always had salty hair? ....

Use more than one adjective in my descriptions

Adjective order

Adjectives make our stories much more interesting. Compare A and B:

A *It was night. The man walked towards the house.*

B *It was a dark stormy night. The exhausted man walked towards the mysterious old house.*

When you use more than one adjective in a description, you need to be careful about the order of the words.

personal opinions   factual information

This is a **famous 16th-century** house.

~~This is a **16th-century famous** house.~~ ✗

It has **beautiful black and white** walls.

It has **unusual wooden** windows.

Some people have seen a **terrifying grey** ghost inside.

You can buy **delicious fresh** snacks from the café.

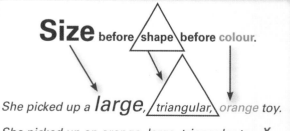

Size before shape before colour.

She picked up a *large, triangular, orange toy.*

~~She picked up an orange, large, triangular toy.~~ ✗
~~She picked up a triangular, orange, large toy.~~ ✗

If there is more than one adjective <u>after</u> the noun and the verb *be* (or *seem, appear, look, feel, become* and others), we need to use *and*.

The necklace was old and red.
~~The necklace was old red.~~ ✗

But, of course, we can say:
It was an old red necklace. ✓

	Personal opinion	Size or length	Physical	Age	Shape	Colour	Origin	Material	Kind or purpose	NOUN
a	wonderful					red				flower
a			heavy					leather	army	jacket
a					round				office	table
a		gigantic		modern			Chinese			painting
a	pretty							cotton		dress
a	well-designed	small	sharp			black		plastic	kitchen	knife

⚠ **This is not a rule! But you will usually be OK if you put adjectives in this order!**

1 Complete the sentences with the adjectives in brackets in the correct order.

a Susie gave me a ___lovely gold___ watch. (gold lovely)

b Gabi cooked some _____ food. (Hungarian delicious)

c The film star had _____ hair. (long blonde)

d It was a _____ frog. (African green small)

e The whole family watched a _____ film. (detective old boring)

f Shelley had a _____ car. (new German pink nice)

g The water in the pool was _____ (warm lovely)

h He wore a _____ coat. (black long horrible)

2 Read the descriptions then write <u>one</u> sentence that has all the information in it.

a It's a clock. It's wooden. It's very old. It's from Switzerland.
It's a very old, wooden, Swiss clock.

b He's young. He's friendly. He's a tennis player.

c I bought a TV. It's Korean. It's new.

d We stared at the statue. It was wonderful. It was ancient. It was made of stone.

e My mother has three cats. They are lovely. They are round. They are large. They are ginger.

f Sandra played a pretty tune on some bells. They were thin. They were long. They were metallic. They were bright red.

3 Describe what you can see in the picture. Use adjectives and nouns from the boxes. (Different answers are possible.)

> brown fat large long ~~modern~~
> red round snowy ~~stone~~ tall

> cow lake mountain ~~statue~~ train

a *a modern stone statue*

b _____

c _____

d _____

e _____

I can ... Talk about people's feelings and opinions

-ed / -ing adjectives

The work is **tiring,**	so Laura feels **tired.**	I was **bored,**	because Alan was so **boring.**
↑ this causes the feelings	↑ this is how Laura feels	↑ this is how I felt	↑ this caused the feeling

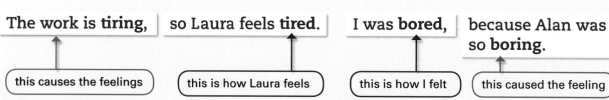

The cause		SO	How the person feels	
It's He's She's	tiring	SO	I feel	tired.
	boring			bored.
	confusing			confused.
	interesting			interested.
	depressing			depressed.
	frightening			frightened.
	surprising			surprised.
	disappointing			disappointed.
	exciting			excited.
	amazing			amazed.
	annoying			annoyed.
	relaxing			relaxed.
	shocking			shocked.
	embarrassing			embarrassed.
	amusing			amused.
	satisfying			satisfied.
	exhausting			exhausted.

⚠ People can be *bored* <u>and/or</u> *boring*!

1 Underline the correct word.

a I don't like this programme. It's really *boring* / *bored*.

b Those children are making a terrible noise. I think it's very *annoying* / *annoyed*.

c This is an important meeting. I'm very *surprising* / *surprised* that you arrived late.

d Listen to this. It's very *relaxing* / *relaxed* music.

e I'll never watch this film again. It always makes me feel *depressing* / *depressed*.

f Are you *interesting* / *interested* in making a lot of money?

g I left Marcia's birthday present at home. It was so *embarrassing* / *embarrassed*.

h I left Marcia's birthday present at home. I was so *embarrassing* / *embarrassed*.

i We love listening to Jorge's stories. He's *interesting* / *interested*.

j We love listening to Jorge's stories. We're really *interesting* / *interested* in them.

2 Underline the correct sentence.

a Susie is looking at a book. You want to ask what she thinks about the book. What do you say?

   1 Is it interesting?   **2** Is it interested?

b You are in a dull meeting. You want to ask your colleague how she feels. What do you say?

   1 Are you boring?   **2** Are you bored?

c Phil is having difficulty with his Maths homework. What do you say?

   1 Is it confusing?   **2** Is it confused?

d Phil is having difficulty with his Maths homework. What do you say?

   1 Are you confusing?   **2** Are you confused?

e Eddie is watching an adventure film. You want to ask him about the film. What do you say?

   1 Is it exciting?   **2** Is it excited?

f It's 11 o'clock at night. Jenny is still at her office desk. When you phone her, you want to ask how she feels. What do you say?

   1 Are you exhausting?   **2** Are you exhausted?

g You are very surprised when your best friend says that she is going to get married. What do you say?

   1 I'm shocking.   **2** I'm shocked.

3 Read the conversation. In each question there is one mistake with an *-ed*/*-ing* adjective. Find the mistakes and write the correct words.

a Mary: Did you go to that show last night?

   Beth: The magic show? Yes! It was amazing. I thought it was really ~~excited~~. *exciting*

b Mary Well, I'm glad you liked it. Jeff told me it was boring.

   Beth: Seriously? He was bored? That's very surprised.

c Mary Yes. He was looking forward to it, but he said he was disappointing. He thought most of the magic tricks weren't very interesting.

d Beth: Well, I wasn't boring at all. The show was quite clever … and very amusing as well. I laughed so much!

e Beth: One trick was really shocking! I was so amazing when the giant rabbit jumped up!

4 ABOUT YOU

Complete the sentences so that they are true. Use one or more words from the box in each sentence.

> annoyed / annoying   bored / ~~boring~~
> embarrassed / embarrassing
> exhausted / exhausting
> interested / interesting

a I think that *vampire films* are very *boring.*

b I think that _____ are very _____

c I feel _____ when _____

d The most _____ member of my family is _____

e I always get _____ when _____

f My friend _____

I can ... Say how 'strong' something is

Adverbs of degree

It's fairly hot.   It's rather hot.   It's really hot.   It's terribly hot.

strong   stronger

It's quite hot.   It's pretty hot.   It's very hot.   It's extremely hot.

Words like *fairly*, *rather* and *really* are called **adverbs of degree**. They are used to make an adjective stronger.

 In these sentences:
- *pretty* does <u>not</u> mean *attractive* or *beautiful*
- *terribly* does <u>not</u> mean *badly*.

Some adverbs of degree can also go with:

other adverbs:

Charlie's walking really slowly.
The choir sang quite loudly.

verbs:

I strongly agree with you.
Robert totally confused me with his explanation.
The building noise completely ruined our holiday.

Note the position after *be* and auxiliary verbs.

The situation is rather complicated.
Everyone has really enjoyed themselves.

Some adverbs of degree make meanings weaker.

I'm almost ready.
(= not completely ready)

Child: *Are we there yet?*
Parent: *We're nearly there.*
(= not completely there)

I feel slightly ill.
(= a little ill – not completely ill)

Parent: *Go and play with Lucas.*
Child: *Do I have to? I hardly know him!*
(= I only know him a little.)

hardly = *very little / almost never / almost not at all*

 If you *hardly* do something, it <u>doesn't</u> mean that you never do it. It means that you do it very little or very rarely or that it is only just possible for you to do it.

We've hardly spoken.		*We have spoken very, very little.*
I've hardly used it.		*I have used it very, very little.*
It's hardly changed at all.	**=**	*There have been almost no changes.*
I can hardly see / hear / read it.		*It is almost impossible for me to see / read / hear.*
I can hardly recognise him.		*It is almost impossible for me to recognise him.*
I can hardly wait!		*It is almost impossible for me to wait (because I am excited!).*

(can) hardly + positive verb *I can hardly wait!* ✓ ~~I can't hardly wait.~~ ✗

hardly ever = **not 'never' ... but almost never**

She hardly ever goes to the supermarket.	**=**	*She almost never goes to the supermarket.*

 The adverb *hardly* has a completely different meaning from the adverb *hard*!
She worked hard all day. = **She did a lot of work all day.**
She hardly worked all day. = **She did almost no work all day.**

1 Put the words in brackets into the sentences in the correct place.

a Their house was ^{very}↗tidy. (very)

b I agree with everything that the managers said. (totally)

c The children are tired. (terribly)

d It's late. We need to go home. (rather)

e Priscilla has finished the gardening. (almost)

f We walked quickly across the square to the ice cream shop. (fairly)

2 Rewrite each sentence using *hardly ever*.

a This machine almost never breaks down.
This machine hardly ever breaks down.

b I almost never visit my grandma.

c Terry plays hockey a lot, but almost never plays football.

d I almost never drive a car.

e Jonah almost never leaves this village.

3 Rewrite each sentence using *hardly*.

a It is almost impossible for me to understand him.
I can hardly understand him.

b This town has changed very little since the 1960s.

c After going to the gym it is almost impossible for me to move my legs!

d He is very shy and talks very little to other children.

4 ***ABOUT***

Think of things in your own life that match the descriptions. (Different answers are possible.)

a Something that is extremely annoying!
My old computer!

b A piece of English grammar that is totally confusing.

c An idea that you strongly agree with.

d A book, song or film that is nearly perfect.

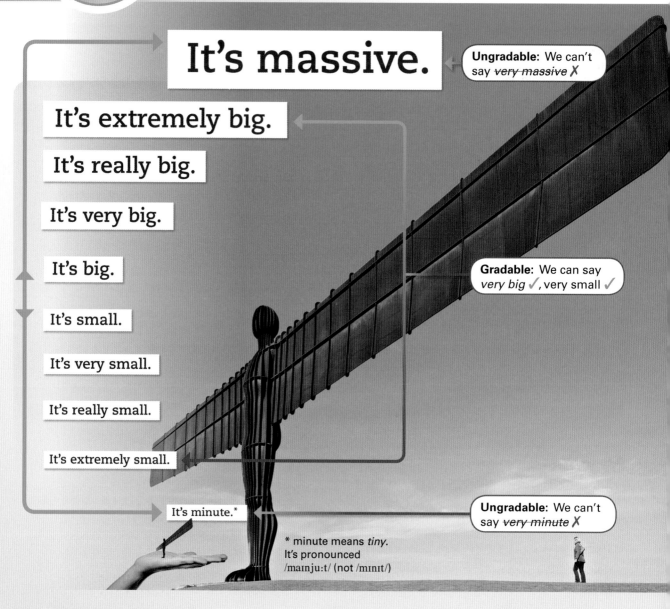

It's massive.

Ungradable: We can't say *very massive* ✗

It's extremely big.

It's really big.

It's very big.

It's big.

Gradable: We can say *very big* ✓, *very small* ✓

It's small.

It's very small.

It's really small.

It's extremely small.

It's minute.*

Ungradable: We can't say *very minute* ✗

* minute means *tiny*.
It's pronounced
/maɪnjuːt/ (not /mɪnɪt/)

Some common ungradable adjectives

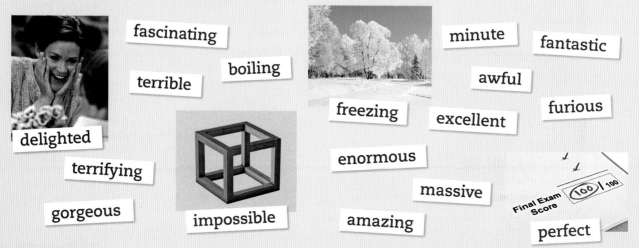

fascinating

minute   fantastic

boiling

terrible   awful

freezing   furious

excellent

delighted

enormous

terrifying

massive

Final Exam Score 100 / 100

gorgeous

impossible   amazing

perfect

Gradable adjectives describe qualities we can measure in degrees.
e.g., *slightly cold, very cold, extremely cold*

Some **ungradable adjectives** are extremes.
e.g. *massive* (= very, very big),
minute (= very, very small)

Some ungradable adjectives are ideas that are impossible to grade!
e.g. *perfect, unique, dead, impossible, married, right, correct*

We can't use the adverbs of degree *very, extremely* and *slightly* with ungradable adjectives

✗ ~~very wonderful, extremely boiling, slightly hilarious~~

but we **can** use

absolutely, totally, completely

✓ *absolutely wonderful, completely amazing, totally hilarious*

really can be used with gradable and ungradable adjectives.

✓ *really cold, really freezing*

1 Underline the correct word.

a That was an *extremely* / <u>*absolutely*</u> wonderful day!
b Their house was *totally* / *very* big.
c The weather was *absolutely* / *very* boiling.
d The rollercoaster ride was *completely* / *very* fantastic.
e The meal was *very* / *really* minute.
f We were *totally* / *very* freezing all afternoon.
g I thought her show was *absolutely* / *very* hilarious.
h This question is *completely* / *very* impossible!
i This question is *completely* / *very* difficult.
j Your homework is *very* / *totally* correct.
k Sanjeev was *very* / *absolutely* angry with Kendra.
l Sanjeev was *very* / *absolutely* furious with Kendra.

3 ABOUT YOU

Complete the sentences so that they are true for you.

a I think that ..*my new phone*.. is ..*absolutely*.. brilliant!
b I think that _____ is _____ hilarious.
c _____ is _____ massive.
d I think that _____ is _____ terrifying.
e _____ is _____ gorgeous.
f My family thinks that _____

2 INTERNET QUIZ

Read the sentences, look at the pictures and check the internet – then complete the sentences.
(Different answers are possible.)

a
The Sahara is absolutely *boiling*.

b
Oymyakon is totally _____

c
MC Escher drew pictures of completely _____ buildings.

d
Behemoth in Ontario, Canada looks absolutely

e
The views in the Lake District, England are really _____

f
Your fingerprints are totally _____

g
Argentinosaurus was absolutely _____

h
The dwarf green tree frog is really _____

More practice

Make my descriptions more interesting

Noun phrases

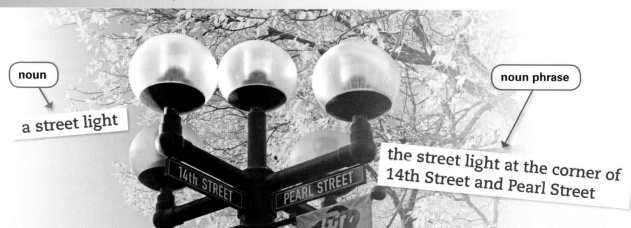

noun

a street light

noun phrase

the street light at the corner of 14th Street and Pearl Street

Nouns

usually one or two words long

a street light   a valley   a remote control   a bottle   a bus stop   sugar

Noun phrases

A group of words, e.g. [article + adjective + noun], which behave like nouns ... but are longer. In these sentences all the <u>underlined</u> words are noun phrases:

Susie looked at <u>some small red books on the second shelf</u>.

<u>The street light at the corner of Pearl Street</u> was on.

I gave <u>my ticket</u> to <u>the woman with long dark hair in the cinema queue</u>.

We can replace a noun phrase with a pronoun:

Susie looked at them.

It was on.

I gave it to her.

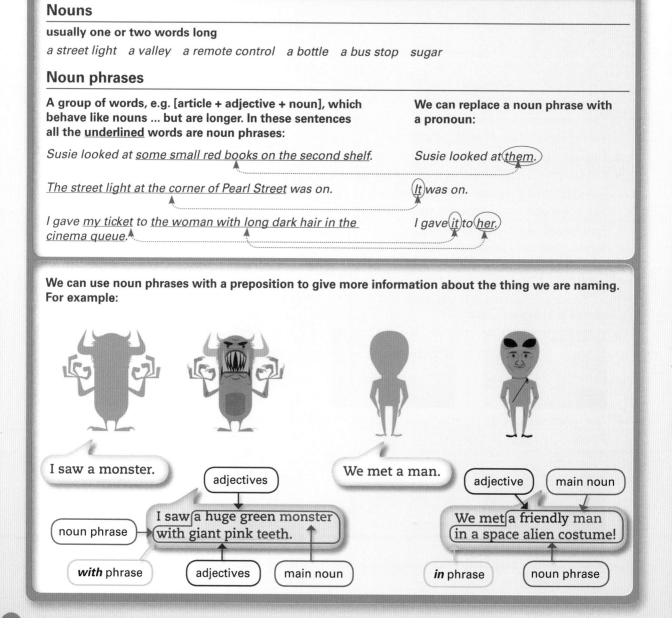

We can use noun phrases with a preposition to give more information about the thing we are naming. For example:

I saw a monster.

adjectives

noun phrase

I saw a huge green monster with giant pink teeth.

with phrase   adjectives   main noun

We met a man.

adjective   main noun

We met a friendly man in a space alien costume!

in phrase   noun phrase

Noun phrases often contain other nouns and noun phrases. Each box here is a noun phrase!

(The street light) at (the corner) of (Pearl Street) was on.

1 Underline the noun phrases in the sentences.

a Inga walked into the small office at the end of the corridor.

b Josie gave him a huge box of expensive chocolates.

c Could you pass me that plate of red peppers, please?

d What's the answer to question 7?

e A very noisy car alarm was going off all night.

f Giovanni won the top prize for athletics last September.

2 Replace each underlined noun phrase with a pronoun.

a That person in the red coat outside the cinema is my mother.

She is my mother.

b She spoke to the rude man behind the desk in Reception.

She spoke to ....

c Could you wash the unwashed dinner plates, please?

....

d I listened carefully to the funny woman with pink hair at the end of the conference.

....

e I bought that ugly old yellow car!

....

f The small cakes on the kitchen table last night were really delicious.

....

g Mike spoke to you, me and all the people in the room.

....

h The loud music at the buffet is very annoying!

....

3 Make the sentences more informative. Use words from the box to make the underlined nouns into noun phrases.

at the end of the street
at the seaside
beautiful classical
delicious
fantastic two-week
full of fresh vegetables from the garden
on its own at the end of the park
on Tom's headphones
rather frightening old
tall
very dark and dirty
with only two other passengers in it

a We went into the _very dark and dirty_ café _at the end of the street._

b Kylie listened to the .... music

....

c Mark cooked a .... soup

....

d The children had a .... holiday

....

e I flew here on a .... plane

....

f Caspar climbed to the top of a .... tree ....

I can ... Describe actions

Adverbs (compared with adjectives)

Adjectives tell us more about **people** and **things**.

Adverbs tell us more about **actions**. They tell us how, when or where something is done.

He's a **wonderful** chef.

The customers are ordering **very slowly**.

I love the **French** food here.

The Petersens **always** arrive **late**.

This steak is **delicious**.

We're working **hard tonight**, aren't we?

I'm very **hungry**.

The chef cooks French food **very well**, doesn't he?

What a **fantastic** meal!

Yes! And he works **fast**!

Adverbs of time tell us <u>when</u> an action happens.

e.g. *yesterday, now, soon, finally, tonight*

There are different kinds of adverb

Adverbs of frequency tell us <u>how often</u> an action is done.

e.g. *often, daily, sometimes, never, usually*

Adverbs of manner tell us <u>how</u> an action is done.

e.g. *carefully, happily, quickly, suddenly, well, hard*

Adverbs of place tell us <u>where</u> an action is done.

e.g. *here, nearby, outside, upstairs, anywhere*

Adverbs of degree tell us <u>how strongly</u> or <u>how much</u> an action is done.

e.g. *very, completely, extremely, quite, hardly*

	Adjective	Adverb
Many adverbs are very similar to adjectives.	happy	happily
	slow	slowly
	angry	angrily
	generous	generously

	Adjective	Adverb
Some are the same!	fast	fast
	hard	hard
	early	early
	late	late
	best	best

	Adjective	Adverb
There is one important one that is completely different.	good	well

1 Draw an arrow from the adjective to the noun or pronoun it tells you more about.

a We worked hard all summer in a huge factory.

b In the morning, Michaela carefully cut the tall grass.

c The lake water was icy, but we happily swam there for ten minutes.

d You did a good job and deserved to win the prize!

e This is my best jacket.

f The early train arrived late.

2 Draw an arrow from the adverb to the verb it tells you more about.

a We worked hard all summer in a huge factory.

b In the morning, Michaela carefully cut the tall grass.

c The lake water was icy, but we happily swam there for ten minutes.

d You worked well and deserved to win the prize!

e I work best on my own.

f The early train arrived late.

3 Make the short descriptions more interesting by adding adjectives and adverbs in some (or all) of the gaps. (Many different answers are possible.)

a Last year we bought an ___old___ house with a ___huge___ garden. Since then, we've worked ___hard___ to tidy and redecorate it.

b The _____ cat walked _____ along the top of the _____ wall. It stopped in front of the _____ tree, then _____ jumped onto a _____ branch.

c The _____ student looked _____ at the exam questions. They seemed very _____ ! She picked up her pen _____ and started to write _____ on the _____ answer paper.

4 **ABOUT** YOU

Complete the sentences so that they are true for you. Use either **one adjective** or **one adverb**. The words in the box may give you some ideas (but feel free to use other words!).

adjectives

> bad clever good hard-working
> helpful lazy popular rude

adverbs

> badly carefully carelessly hard
> quickly slowly ~~well~~

a I want to do this exercise ___well.___

b I'm a _____ student.

c I work _____

d I usually do these exercises _____

e My best friend is quite _____

f I usually sleep _____

g I eat _____

h My family say that I am very _____

More practice

I can ...

Ask and answer about large quantities

much, many, a lot of, lots of, loads of, plenty of

There isn't **much** space on this shelf.

There are **lots of** microwaves on shelf 679K.

We don't have **many** kettles.

We've got **plenty of** toasters.

Hurry up with that order! We haven't got **much** time!

I've got a headache. There's **so much** noise!

How many people work here?

How much money do they earn?

Do you use **a lot of** robots?

Does this place use **a lot of** electricity?

Do they make **loads of** mistakes?

---

a lot of = lots of = loads of (*loads of* is more informal)

We don't usually use *a lot of* / *lots of* / *loads of* with amounts of time or distance.

They travelled for ~~lots of~~ many kilometres.
Charlotte stayed with us for ~~lots of~~ many days.

plenty of = a large amount (perhaps more than enough or too much!)
We had plenty of food for the party.

We can use *so much* and *so many* in positive sentences to talk about a large amount of something in an emphatic way.

We had so much fun!
There were so many people in town.

We use *How much* and *How many* to ask about quantities.

How much money have you got?
How many sandwiches did you buy?

with plural nouns

	positive	negative	question
many	(✓) *Many adults enjoy video games.*	✓ *I don't know many people.*	✓ *Have you got many DVDs?*
much	✗	✗	✗
a lot of lots of loads of plenty of	✓ *I've got loads of friends.*	✓ *I don't know a lot of people.* (except ✗ *plenty*)	✓ *Have you got lots of DVDs?*

✓ = good
✗ = not possible
(✓) = possible – but be careful! Mainly used when *many* is the subject. In other sentences, use *a lot of / lots of / loads of.* '*I have lots of ideas*' sounds more natural than '*I have many ideas*'.

with uncountable nouns

	positive	negative	question
many	✗	✗	✗
much	✗ (except ✓ *so much*)	✓ *I don't have much information.*	✓ *Have you got much time?*
a lot of lots of loads of plenty of	✓ *I've got loads of experience.*	✓ *I don't have a lot of information.* (except ✗ *plenty*)	✓ *Have you got plenty of time?*

1 Complete the sentences with *lots of, many* or *much*. (Different answers may be possible.)

a The birds made ___lots of___ noise outside their cabin every morning.

b How _____ people will be at the meeting tomorrow?

c Was there _____ traffic this morning?

d Have you seen? There are _____ people waiting outside your office.

e Your class has made so _____ progress over the last year.

f Our spaceship travelled _____ kilometres to get to the asteroid.

g The children didn't have _____ enthusiasm for their new project.

h Sorry, but I don't have _____ information about the conference.

i I didn't see _____ rare birds in the nature park.

j How _____ pocket money do the children get each week?

k This place is awful! There's _____ noise!

l When the detectives searched his room, they found _____ diamonds in old food boxes.

2 Make questions with *how many* or *how much*.

a I ate a lot of cakes last night!
How many (cakes) did you eat?

b Aunt Alma gave the children a lot of money.

c We bought some sandwiches.

d The climbers took some water with them to the camp.

e The climbers took some water bottles with them to the camp.

f *InterWorld Shipping* paid very little tax last year.

g The boys sold lots of cards for charity.

h The boys made lots of money for charity.

all, every, most, the whole, several, a couple, none, both, a few, a little, no

Yesterday afternoon hundreds of people drove to see the big game at the stadium, but ...

... all the cars were caught in a huge traffic jam.

all (of) the + plural OR uncountable = 100%

Every road in the town centre was completely jammed.

The **whole** town centre was affected.

every + singular = 100%

the whole (of the) + singular = 100%

SPORTS NEWS

None of the traffic was moving.

none of the + plural OR uncountable = 0

Several drivers abandoned their vehicles and walked.

several (of the) + plural = more than 2, but not many

A **couple** of drivers started fighting.

Both men were hot and angry.

a couple of (the) + plural = 2

both (of the) + plural = 2 previously mentioned people or things

A **few** motorbikes were stuck too ...

... but **most** of them escaped onto the pavement.

Fortunately, there were **no** accidents.

a few (of the) + plural OR
a little (of the) + uncountable = a small quantity, more than 0

most (of the) + plural OR uncountable = more than 50%

no + plural OR uncountable = 0

Does *of the* change the meaning? Yes!

A few children are very noisy.
(= children in general, everywhere, all the time)

A few of the children are very noisy.
(= the children we are talking about, e.g. here, now)

Most people like Abba!
(= people in general, everywhere, all the time)

Most of the people like Abba!
(= the people we are talking about, e.g. at a party)

all of	a few of	
most of	both of	**+** you / us / them
several of	none of	

I met the two new recruits. Both of them seemed very keen.

Many of us are worried about the new plans.

All of the flowers grew quickly.

or ... *my, your, her,* etc. or ... *John's, Jennifer's,* etc. or ... *these, those*

e.g. *All of our flowers grew quickly.*

1 Underline the sentences which are good descriptions of the picture.

bouncy castle

swing

slide

roundabout

a 1 <u>There are several children on the roundabout</u>.
  2 All the children are on the roundabout.
b 1 A few men are jumping on the bouncy castle.
  2 Both men are jumping on the bouncy castle.
c 1 There is a little food on the tables.
  2 There is plenty of food on the tables.
d 1 A couple of women are looking at a baby.
  2 Most of the women are looking at a baby.
e 1 There's a little rubbish by the bouncy castle.
  2 There's no rubbish by the bouncy castle.
f 1 Most of the children are playing on the slide.
  2 A few of the children are playing on the slide.
g 1 A few of the women are eating the food.
  2 None of the women are eating the food.

2 Look at the pictures. Say how many of the eggs are broken. (Different answers are possible.)

a    **b**

Most of the eggs are broken.

c   **d**

e   **f**

3 Complete the sentences. Use the words in the box.

both   couple   my   of   ~~several~~   the   them

a I went to a great conference last week. I met
  several   new contacts.
b I've tried lots of pairs of shoes, but none of
  .... really fitted me.
c I'm going to have a party and I want all ....
  best friends to come.
d Most of .... people in our office are women.
e Have some more! There's plenty .... food!
f I met an old friend at the match and .... of
  us went to have a curry together afterwards.
g Beatrice checked her wallet and found that she
  only had a .... of business cards left.

More practice

I can ... Refer to things without repeating their name

one, ones

> There are lots of strange guns and weapons.

> What are those **ones** for?

> Wow! I want some of these souvenirs! Which **ones** do you fancy?

> Have you seen that guard? The **one** with the sword!

> Look! Fantastic fish!

> Those large posters are great. I'm going to get **one**.

> The red **ones** are the prettiest!

> I've bought a guidebook. Do you want **one**?

When you have just used a noun (e.g. *guidebook, pen, fish,* etc.), it's better not to repeat exactly the same noun again straight away. (It's not 'wrong' – it just sounds less interesting!)

I've got an iPad. Have you got <u>an iPad</u>?

Instead, we can use *one*.

*I've got an iPad. Have you got **one**?*

The word *one* refers back to the earlier noun and means 'a similar example'.

One can refer back to a whole noun phrase.

*We need <u>a very large piece of paper</u>. Andy's got **one** on his desk.*

*Did you see that <u>beautiful tropical plant</u>? I've got **one** at home.*

We can use *ones* to refer back to plural nouns and noun phrases.

*There are lots of <u>sweets</u> here. Which **ones** do you want?*

⚠️ We can't use *one* or *ones* to refer back to uncountable nouns.

This rice is delicious. ~~Would you like one?~~ ✗
This rice is delicious. Would you like some? ✓

We can say:
the one ✓
the ones ✓
this one ✓
that one ✓
these ones ✓
those ones ✓
which ones? ✓
my one / your one / her one, **etc.** ✓

adjective + *one / ones*
e.g. *a green one / the small one / expensive ones / square ones,* **etc.** ✓

We can't say:
~~a one~~ ✗ **e.g.** *~~Let's buy a guidebook. We need a one with a map inside.~~* ✗
Let's buy a guidebook. We need one with a map inside. ✓

~~two ones~~ ✗   *~~three ones~~* ✗   *~~four ones~~,* **etc.** ✗
~~some ones~~ ✗   *~~any ones~~* ✗

1 In each question write *one* or *ones* instead of the repeated noun or noun phrase.

a Oh, look! A lucky waving cat!
I've got ~~a lucky waving cat~~ at home.
 ᴧ *one*

b Is this computer better than that computer?

c These cakes are amazing! Which cakes do you want to take home?

d This is the car park. My car is the red car over there.

e Ah look – this room has some ancient Egyptian statues. Yes, these are the ancient Egyptian statues the museum guidebook was talking about.

f Are you having dancing lessons with Miss Gable? The dancing lessons with Miss Gable I went to last year were boring.

g Did you buy a new phone charger? The new phone chargers I saw in the supermarket looked very poor quality – but the new phone chargers in the Dudley street market are really good. In fact, I bought a new phone charger there myself! Would you like to get a new phone charger now?

3 Each time that Ella uses *one / ones* she gets something wrong. Correct the mistakes.

a I need a hammer. Have you got ~~ones~~?
 ....*one*........

b You need lots of flour in this recipe. Have you got ~~one~~? ....*some*........

c I love those flowers. The purple one are so pretty! ....

d There are twenty reports on the table. I want each person to take ones and read it before the meeting. ....

e My calculator has broken. Can I borrow a one from you? ....

f Are you looking for laptop bags? I've got two ones next to my desk. ....

g It's not fair. Susie has got seven sweets, but I haven't got any ones. ....

2 There is a stall selling cakes at school. Complete the sentences to show which student wants which cake, using *one* or *ones* and the words in the box.

> big   blue   ~~chocolate~~   pink   with a cherry on top
> with fresh cream   ~~with sprinkles~~   with strawberries   yellow

a Charlie wants a *chocolate one.*

b David wants *one with sprinkles.*

c Sam can't decide between a .... and a ....

d Wendy wants a ....

e Bill and Maggie both want ....

f Freddy would like ....

g Sue wants .... and ....

Indefinite pronouns: **someone**, **somebody**, **something**, **not + anyone**, **not + anybody**, **not + anything**, **no one**, **nobody**, **nothing**

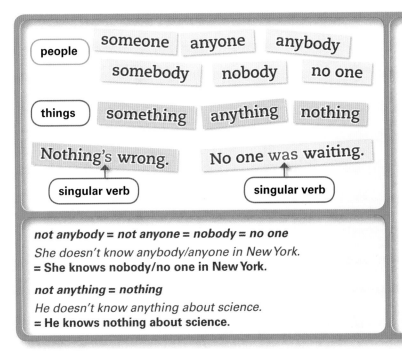

No one / nobody / nothing go with positive verbs. Don't use them with a negative verb.

Angelina told nobody about the meeting. ✓

~~*Angelina didn't tell nobody about the meeting.*~~ ✗

We can use **anyone / anybody / anything** as the subject of positive statements and questions, but not when we make a negative.

Anyone can tell you the answer. ✓

Can anyone tell you the answer? ✓

~~*Anyone can't tell you the answer.*~~ ✗

not anybody = not anyone = nobody = no one
She doesn't know anybody/anyone in New York.
= She knows nobody/no one in New York.

not anything = nothing
He doesn't know anything about science.
= He knows nothing about science.

1 Complete the sentences with *nobody* or *nothing*.

a *Nobody* knows how many tigers still live in India.

b Candy checked the envelope, but there was .... in it.

c I worked hard all afternoon in his garden. What do you think he gave me? .... !

d These houses are all empty. .... has lived here since the 1990s.

e Why did you buy broccoli? .... likes broccoli!

f I'm sorry I can't help you. I'm afraid there is .... I can do.

g We waited for more than an hour, but .... came to meet us.

2 Complete the sentences with *nobody* or *anybody*.

a Would *anybody* like a cup of tea?

b We've all tried, but .... could open this box! Can you do it?

c Steve went to his house, but there wasn't .... at home.

d I can't do question 6! Does .... know the answer?

e .... has volunteered for the night shift.

f Greg knows .... in Kuala Lumpur.

g Greg doesn't know .... in Kuala Lumpur.

3 Underline the correct verb for each sentence.

a No one in our house *like / doesn't like / likes* pizza!

b If anyone *want / wants* to see the agenda, there are copies on the desk.

c Someone *is shouting / are shouting* in the street.

d The police searched every room. No one *was / wasn't / were* there.

e *Have / Has* anyone phoned while I was out?

f This is a really boring town. Nothing *happen / doesn't happen / happens* here.

g It's so unfair! Nobody *understand / doesn't understand / understands* me!

4 Complete the sentences with the words in the box.

anybody anything ~~no one~~ nothing
someone something

a Kelly arrived in the office at the correct time, but it was empty. *No one* was there.

b Tom said that he couldn't help because he knew .... about car engines.

c The teacher counted the students. 'Why are there only 39?' she asked. '.............. is missing!'

d I want to watch the film tonight, so please don't tell me .... about it.

e When Mick came into the room, he could immediately see that there was a problem. .... was wrong.

f 'Sorry. The tax office is closed today. There isn't .... who can answer your call. Please try again tomorrow.'

Name groups of people

Collective nouns

people

a member of
the audience

a man

a woman

the audience

a child

a businesswoman

the CEO

a salesman

the company

the head of marketing

managers

soldier

soldier

soldier

sergeant

the army

soldier

student

student

student

our class

teacher

students

Dad

Mum

our family

Cheryl

Mike

policemen

the police

policeman

policewoman

policewomen

Some words have a meaning that includes many different people. They are called **collective nouns**.

For example, *an audience* in the theatre has many people in it.

When we talk about the audience, we can:

- use a *singular* verb if we are thinking of the whole group of people as ONE THING.
  The audience is very quiet.
- use a plural verb if we are thinking about all the different individual people in the audience.
  The audience are standing, laughing, shouting and clapping.
- **we always use a plural verb with *the police*.**

ALL the class together	singular verb

After lunch break, **the class** always goes to the library.

DIFFERENT people doing DIFFERENT things.	plural verb

After school finishes, **the class** go to their clubs or sports, or go home.

But ... don't worry too much! It's usually OK to use either singular or plural verbs because the difference in meaning is very small.

Some common collective nouns.

army   audience   band   choir   class   company   crowd   department

family   gang   government   group   police   school   team

---

1 Replace the <u>underlined</u> words with a collective noun.

a The singers were nervous, but the <u>people watching in the theatre</u> loved it.   *audience*

b Mrs Andrews told the <u>students who study together in the same room</u> to be quiet.

c The <u>11 footballers wearing the same colour clothes</u> ran onto the field shouting.

d The <u>group of people who sing together</u> gave a wonderful Christmas concert last year.

e We planned to go to see the celebrations by the river, but there was a large <u>group of people in the same place</u> so we decided to watch it at home on TV.

f The <u>group of people who make decisions and control this country</u> has raised income tax again!

g The sales and marketing <u>group of people who work together in one part of this company</u> are going on a team-building break this weekend.

2 **ABOUT** YOU

Choose a collective noun in each sentence. Then complete the sentences so that they are true for you and your life.

a My class / ~~team / department~~
  are all improving in English.

b My team / gang / group

c In our school / department / company

d In my country the government / police / army

OK, let me tell you who everyone is.

Mrs Ashe is the old woman sitting at the table.

Her daughter is the young woman looking out of the window.

Can you see the men walking and talking by the fountain? They're going to come inside now.

The tall man standing near the door – that's the hero, Mr Derby. Yes, the one holding a hat. He's going to walk over to the young woman and tell her he loves her.

Mrs Ashe is the old woman.

Which old woman?

The old woman *sitting at the table*.

We can say <u>exactly</u> which person we are talking about by saying <u>what they are doing</u>.

⚠ **No auxiliary verb!**

Which man?

The man ~~is~~ standing next to the tree.

We can use this structure in longer sentences and questions.

Do you know the man speaking on the phone?

The boys playing in the garden are Jenny's sons.

That dog barking outside is very annoying!

We can also use this structure to talk about things.

The camera standing by the door is for close-ups.

The taxi coming up the drive is for you.

1 Decide which person is being talked about.

a	the man holding a newspaper	*Person 3*
b	the woman looking at her watch	
c	the person standing next to the tree	
d	the person leaning against the wall	
e	the person smiling at the child	
f	the person pickpocketing the tourist	
g	the person looking for his wallet	

2 Look at this picture. This time, it's your job to describe the people!

a	Person 1	*the woman speaking on the phone*
b	Person 2	
c	Person 3	
d	Person 4	
e	Person 5	
f	Person 6	
g	Person 7	

More practice

Identify a person or thing by giving more information about them or it

Relative clauses with **who**, **that**, **where** and **which**

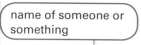

name of someone or something		the kind of creature or thing it is	• **who** or **that** for people (and creatures) • **that** or **which** for things • **where** for places	what it is or does
A telepath	is	a person	who	reads other people's minds.
A gas giant	is	a planet	that	is very large and made of gas.
Helleconia	is	a planet	where	each season lasts for hundreds of years.

If we can't find a good word for the kind of creature or thing ... we can use *someone, something, a thing*.

A chef is someone who cooks meals in a restaurant.

An alarm is something that makes a very loud noise to warn you of danger.

A hole punch is a thing that makes holes in pieces of paper.

1 A five-year-old is asking you some questions. Use words from A and B to help you complete the answers.

A

cream   famous person   ~~machine~~   people
person   piece of metal   place   tool

B

~~chops food~~
cuts wood
dances in the theatre
helps your skin
holds pieces of paper together
people borrow books
serve your food in a restaurant
wrote plays

a What's a food processor?
A food processor is a *machine that chops food.*

b What's a ballet dancer?
A ballet dancer is a

c What's a paper clip?
A paper clip is a

d What's a library?
A library is a

e What's a saw?
A saw is a

f Who was Shakespeare?
Shakespeare was a

g What's moisturiser?
Moisturiser is a

h What are waiters?
Waiters are

2 Answer the questions. Use *who*, *that* or *where* in each sentence.

a What's a ticket inspector?
A ticket inspector is a person who checks your
tickets on a train.

b What's a cinema?

c Who was Mozart?

d What's an iPod?

e What's an alien?

f What's a dishwasher?

3 INTERNET QUIZ 🔍

There are two mistakes in each sentence!
(i) The word *that* has been left out. Write *who* or *that* in the correct position. (ii) The names have been mixed up. Put the correct name in each sentence.

        The Titanic   *that*
a The Kon-Tiki ⋀ was the ship ⋀ hit an iceberg in the Atlantic and sank.

b Betsy Ross   was the woman studied chimpanzees.

c John Logie Baird was the man discovered oxygen.

d ~~The Titanic~~   was the spaceship took the first men to the Moon.

e Joseph Priestley was the man invented TV.

f Jane Goodall   was the woman made the first US flag.

g The Eagle   was the wooden ship crossed the Pacific Ocean.

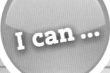

Identify a person by giving more information about them

Relative clauses with **who**

| The man is a computer engineer. | **+** | He recommended the THS45X. |

The man **who recommended the THS45X** is a computer engineer.

(Add **who**) (No **he**)

| I've met the artists. | **+** | They painted *Night Lightning*. |

= I've met the artists **who painted *Night Lightning*.**

(Add **who**) (No **they**)

The part of the sentence starting with *who* is **a relative clause**.

The word *who* is **a relative pronoun**.

We can use *that* instead of *who*. It means exactly the same.

This is the singer that / who wrote Terrible Skies.

---

1 Join the two sentences using *who*.

a We watched a film about a pirate. He stole a ship.
  We watched a film about a pirate who stole a ship.

b I met a girl. She knew lots of pop stars.

....

c The policeman had a red badge. He asked me lots of questions.

....

d We employed a plumber. He had good recommendations.

....

e Some guards were working all night. They heard the alarm at 2 a.m.

....

f At the centre of the ancient temple we met a wise man. He told us a secret.

....

g The soldiers worked all night. They were building the well.

....

h Mariel got a text message from a boy. She met him yesterday.

....

2 INTERNET QUIZ 🔎

Write endings to these sentences with *who*. Use words from the two boxes. Check the internet to help you.

```
discovered   invented   killed
ruled   sailed   took
```

```
a historic bus ride   Egypt from 51 to 30 BC
Julius Caesar   non-stop round the world
the Caesar salad   the wreck of the Titanic
```

a Cleopatra was the woman
  who ruled Egypt from 51 to 30 BC.

b Marcus Junius Brutus was the man

....

c Caesar Cardini was the man

....

d Robert Duane Ballard was the man

....

e Rosa Parks was the woman

....

f Robin Knox-Johnston was the person

....

 More practice

(**who** is the subject of the verb **won**) (When **who** is the subject, we <u>cannot</u> leave it out. We **must** have the relative pronoun.)

The woman **who won** the TV quiz last night lives in our town. ✓

~~The woman won the TV quiz last night lives in our town.~~ ✗

(**who** is **NOT** the subject of the verb **told**) (Tom is the person that told you ... SO ... **Tom** is the subject of the verb **told**.)

This is the woman **who** Tom **told** you about. ✓

(When **who** is NOT the subject, we <u>can</u> leave it out.)

This is the woman Tom **told** you about. ✓

(No **who**!)

⚠ In all these sentences, we can use *that* instead of *who*.

1 In seven sentences, write *who* in the correct place. In one sentence you do not need *who*. Which sentence?

a In the film, Keira plays a woman $\overset{who}{\wedge}$ falls in love with a mountaineer.

b In the middle of the car park I saw a woman was sitting on top of her car!

c Please pass the microphone to the man put up his hand.

d Harriet is an old lady has lived in the hotel for more than 20 years.

e I've met lots of people really like the song.

f People live outside their own country often miss their favourite food.

g That's the man Jane told us about.

h This club was started by people want to keep the old railway open.

2 Join the two sentences. Use *who* or *that*, but leave out *who* or *that* if it is possible.

a I saw two guards. They were standing in front of the main entrance.
I saw two guards that were standing in front of the main entrance.

b He's the person. I gave money to him.
He's the person I gave money to.

c I'd like you to introduce to a man. He parachuted off the Eiffel Tower!

....

d I saw three people. They were getting ready to play tennis.

....

e Oh listen – this is the singer. I recommended her to our class last week.

....

f The rescuers found a dog. He survived the tornado.

....

g This is the famous dog. I wrote a newspaper article about him.

....

h These are the children. I told a ghost story to them.

....

i The children asked for a ghost story. The children arrived early.

....

More practice

I can ...

Say which thing I'm talking about

Relative clauses with **that** or **which**

Wow! You're selling a lot of stuff. Where did it all come from?

Well ... These are some books **which** I've already read.

Those are hats **that** I don't wear any more.

This is a lamp **that** my grandma gave me.

This is the suitcase **which** I took to India last year.

lamp

suitcase

books

hats

YARD SALE

And that's a scooter **that** I rode when I was a child. I'm too big for it now!

scooter

We can give more information about something using **that**. It's like joining two sentences together.

These are some books.   **+**   I've already read them.

=

These are some books that I've already read.

Add **that**   No **them**

⚠ **Common mistake:** *These are some books that I've already read* ~~them~~. ✗

We can use **which** instead of *that*. **Which** can only be used to talk about things, not people. (**Which** is less common than *that*.)

This is the email from my landlord.   **+**   It explains everything.

=

This is the email from my landlord which explains everything.

Add **which**   No **it**

Word order:

The bread is delicious **+** You made it yesterday.

=

The bread that you made yesterday is delicious.

The underlined part is a **noun phrase**. It behaves like one noun.

The part of the sentence starting with *that* or *who* is **a relative clause**.

That is a **relative pronoun**.

When *that* or *which* is the subject, we cannot leave it out.

This is the car which broke down last week. ✓

This is the car broke down last week. ✗

When *that* or *which* is NOT the subject, we can leave it out.

I bought the car that we looked at last week. ✓

I bought the car we looked at last week. ✓

1 Write *that* in the correct place in each sentence.

a Where's the book ∧ I put on the table last night?
    that

b This is the train goes to Glasgow.

c This is a great smartphone app counts all the calories in your food.

d I can't stand cafés have very loud music.

e This is the CCTV camera stopped working.

f He sang a funny song about a dog won first prize in a dog show.

g What did you do with the money Gabriela gave you?

2 Join the two sentences using *that*.

a There's the hairbrush. I lost it last week!
There's the hairbrush that I lost last week!

b This is the report. I promised to write it.

c Here are the second-hand toys. Marilyn gave them to the nursery.

d Did you watch the TV programme? It had a million-dollar prize.

e The apples are bad. You bought them last week.

f Has anyone seen the glove? I left it here this morning.

g All the work was useless. We did the work.

h The lake is beautiful. It is in the middle of the park.

3 In England children like to play 'I Spy' (= 'I can see'). Can you think of a possible answer for each question? (Different answers are possible.)

a I spy … something that is green.   *grass*

b I spy … something that is made of plastic.

c I spy … something that has four wheels.

d I spy … something that is very heavy.

4 Write some 'I Spy' sentences for these answers.

a I spy *something that is very hot.* (the Sun)

b I spy .... (a window)

c I spy .... (a shoe)

d I spy .... (a calculator)

5 **ABOUT** YOU

Complete the sentences so that they are true for you.

a I enjoy films that *don't have a happy ending.*

b I like music which ....

c I can't stand TV programmes that ....

d I .... computers that ....

e I .... pets that ....

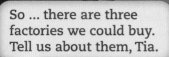

So ... there are three factories we could buy. Tell us about them, Tia.

A

B

C

Factory A is small. It produces 2,000 units a day.

Factory B is **a little bigger than** Factory A. The workforce is **much larger**, so it produces **more units**. However, each unit will be **more expensive**. So this factory is **less economical**.

Factory C is **the most modern building** and it has **the fewest workers**. This factory has **the most experience** at making these products.

OK, OK ... but which one do you think we should buy?

Well ... A is good. B is **better**. C is definitely **the best**.

	Comparative (Comparing things)	**Superlative** (Saying that something is the 'most' or 'least')
	+ -er (shorter words) more / less (longer words)	the + -est (shorter words) the most / the least (longer words)
small	**smaller** (+ -er)	**the smallest** (+ -est)
large	**larger** (ending in e: + r)	**the largest** (ending in e: + st)
big	**bigger** (double consonant + -er)	**the biggest** (double consonant + -est)
tiny	**tinier** (y → ier)	**the tiniest** (y → iest)
expensive	**more expensive** **less expensive**	**the most expensive** **the least expensive**
good	**better** (irregular)	**the best** (irregular)
bad	**worse** (irregular)	**the worst** (irregular)

We can compare one person or thing with another using *than*.

Ted is older than Sylvia.

We can also make good sentences without *than*.

This newsagent's was opened in 1920. The greengrocer's is older.

Use *much / a great deal / a lot / far* if you think there is a big difference.

It's much worse than Factory B.
This book is a great deal longer than I expected.
This cake is a lot sweeter!
The new tower is far taller than the old one.

Use *even* to add emphasis.

My salary is small. Yours is even smaller.

Use *a little / a bit / slightly* if you think there is a small difference.

It's a little bigger than Factory A.
She's a bit older than her cousin.
The children are slightly happier this evening.

We can compare adverbs as well as adjectives. Use *more / less* or *most / least*.

He walked more slowly after his skiing accident.
The City 7 bus stops here most frequently. The Express 12 comes less often.

We can use comparatives and superlatives in front of nouns.

The younger child passed all her exams.
Tina gave more humorous answers than the others.
I think this is the smallest smartphone I've ever seen.
She's the best singer in this year's competition.

1 Complete the table.

Adjective	Comparative	Superlative
strong	a *stronger*	the strongest
happy	b	the happiest
exciting	more exciting	c
wide	d	the widest
e	worse	f
popular	less popular	g
wet	h	i
j	k	the best
attractive	l	m
few	n	o
nice	p	q
busy	r	s
close	t	u

2 Complete the sentences with the correct form of the words in the box.

~~big~~ crowded dark exciting
old small tasty

a This house is large, but that one is much *bigger.*
b Your office is tiny, but mine is even ....
c This soup is nice, but the one your aunt made was a lot ....
d Your DVD looks quite interesting, but I think this one might be ....
e There are lots of people in this classroom, but I think that room 2C is even ....
f Mr McTavish was 90 last birthday, but I think that Mrs Taylor is even ....
g I like that paint – but it's very bright. I prefer this .... colour.

3 For each question, choose a suitable phrase from the box and make a superlative using *-est, most* or *least*.

a horrible noise   a hot summer
a rainy summer   a successful student
an expensive thing   ~~an interesting article~~
an untidy room

a Did you really enjoy reading this? It's so boring! In fact, I think it's *the least interesting article* in the whole newspaper.
b What a terrible mess! I can't even walk through the door! This is .... I've ever seen.
c I asked her what she'd like. She chose a diamond necklace! It was .... in the whole shop.
d Yes, I'm afraid Tom failed six of the tests. He was .... in his class.
e We had a terrible holiday in 2011. It rained every day. The TV said it was .... for twenty years.
f We had a fantastic sunny seaside holiday in 2013. The newspaper said it was .... for many years.
g What a terrible concert! The Robot Army were awful! It was .... I've ever heard.

More practice

Say that some things are 'less' than others

not as … as

Dinah's working hard. She's busy.

Sheldon has a lot of work. He's very busy.

Sheldon's busier than Dinah.

These mean the same!

Dinah isn't as busy as Sheldon.

The Burj Khalifa <u>is taller than</u> the Empire State Building.

The Empire State Building <u>isn't as tall as</u> the Burj Khalifa.

You're getting old!

I'm <u>not as old as</u> you!

Ah! We aren't <u>as strong as</u> we were!

1 Write the comparisons. Use *-er than* / *more than* or *not as … as* and a word from the box.

> ~~big~~ bright cold damaged
> expensive ~~heavy~~ old tall

a

Box X *isn't as big as Box Y.*

b

Box Y *is heavier than Box X.*

c

Box X ....

d

Box X ....

e
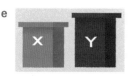
Box Y ....

f

Box X ....

g
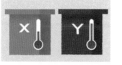
Box X ....

h

Box Y ....

2 Rewrite the second sentence so that it means the same as the first.

a *Batman* is more frightening than *Twilight*.
Twilight isn't *as frightening as Batman.*

b *War and Peace* is longer than *The Little Prince*!
The Little Prince isn't ....

c My dinner isn't as tasty as your dinner.
Your dinner is ....

d Sophie answered more questions than Mike.
Mike didn't answer ....

e My new phone isn't as good as my old one.
My old phone was ....

f This week, class 6B's work was worse than class 6A's.
This week, class 6A's work wasn't ....

3 INTERNET QUIZ 🔍

Make sentences with *not as … as*. Use the internet to check information.

a Rio / Reykjavik / hot
Reykjavik isn't as hot as Rio.

b Panama Canal / Suez Canal / long

c panthers / cheetahs / fast

d Great Zimbabwe / Machu Picchu / old

e Arctic / Antarctic / cold

More practice

as ... as

I can bounce really high!

So can I! I can bounce **as** high **as** you!

as ... as means that something is the same as (or very similar to) another thing

Comparing actions

adverbs				
I can jump		high		you.
I did my homework	as	well	as	everyone else!
We walked		far		possible.

Comparing people and things

adjectives				
This machine is		good		that one.
The XB7 processor is		fast		the IB32.
She's	as	clever	as	someone twice her age.
It's		hot		the Sahara in here!
My dog is		fat		yours (or your dog).

Many common expressions use *as ... as*.

This Maths homework is really difficult. I'll do <u>as much as possible</u>.

Help yourself to the food! Take <u>as much as you want</u>!

Get here <u>as soon as possible</u>!

I'll go <u>as fast as I can</u>.

<u>As far as I remember</u>, this film's really good. **(= I may be wrong, but I think I remember.)**

Many idioms use *as ...as*.

The baby was <u>as good as gold</u>. **(= very well-behaved)**

Your car is <u>as old as the hills</u>. **(= very old)**

The old lady was <u>as quiet as a mouse</u>. **(= very quiet)**

The celebrity was <u>as cool as a cucumber</u>. **(= very relaxed and 'cool')**

That new tool was <u>as useful as a chocolate teapot</u>! **(= completely useless)**

He was so embarrassed! His face went <u>as red as a beetroot</u>! **(= very red)**

1 Two small children are talking. Every time Maisie says something, Marnie says that it's the same for her! Write her sentences.

Maisie: I can jump very high.
Marnie: *I can jump as high as you!* .... a
Maisie: I work really hard!
Marnie: .... b
Maisie: I do my homework carefully.
Marnie: c
Maisie: I get up early on Saturdays.
Marnie: .... d
Maisie: My school's big.
Marnie: .... e
Maisie: My dad plays the guitar brilliantly.
Marnie: .... f

2 Match the sentence halves.

a The boys behaved well. They were ●
b My granny bought her computer in 1997. It's
c When I realised my mistake, I went
d I don't want to be late. We need to leave
e George's surname is Lazarus,
f I hope I'll get this report finished. I'm working

1 as red as a beetroot.
2 as good as gold.
3 as hard as I can.
4 as old as the hills.
5 as soon as possible.
6 as far as I remember.

This is **such a great idea** for a holiday! I love this town!

It's **so hot that** you could fry an egg on the pavement.

This tram's moving **so slowly**! We could walk faster!

It's **so awful that** I can't eat it.

HOT DOGS

He cooked it **so badly**!

The last day! I can't believe it's time to go home! It went **so quickly**!

Come and look! It's **such a beautiful sunset**.

I'm **so tired that** I need a holiday!

Use SO + adjective or adverb to add emphasis.

It's hot! → *It's **SO** hot!*   *He cooked it badly.* → *He cooked it **SO** badly.*

> The meaning is stronger than the adjective on its own.

> The meaning is stronger than the adverb on its own.

Often, we pronounce the word *so* with extra stress – a bit louder, longer and higher in pitch.
*I'm **SO** tired!*

Use SO + adjective or adverb + *that* to say what happens because something is very extreme.

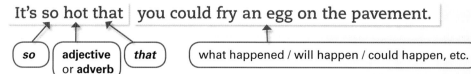

It's so hot that | you could fry an egg on the pavement.

so | **adjective** or **adverb** | *that* | what happened / will happen / could happen, etc.

> *such a* + adjective + noun has a similar meaning to *so* + adjective.
>
> *It's such a beautiful sunset.* = **The sunset is so beautiful.**
>
> *That's such a good idea!* = **That idea is so good.**
>
> **We can also use *that* to say what happens as a result.**
>
> *It was such an amazing dream that I wrote it down when I woke up.*

1 Underline the correct adjective or adverb in each sentence.

a He ran the race so *quick* / *quickly* that he beat the world record.

b That was such a *strange* / *strangely* story!

c The visitor behaved so *strange* / *strangely*.

d Oh, I'm so angry with myself! It was such a *stupid* / *stupidly* mistake!

e Thank you! You gave the school such a *generous* / *generously* present!

f Thank you! You are so *generous* / *generously*!

g Thank you! You gave so *generous* / *generously*!

h Do you have to play so *noisy* / *noisily*?

i It happened so *sudden* / *suddenly*!

j You did that job so *good* / *well*.

k You did such a *good* / *well* job.

2 Complete the sentences using *so* + an adjective from the box.

> cheap glad hilly keen
> ~~quiet~~ sad tiring

a It's ___so quiet___ in here. Why isn't anyone talking?

b These bags are .... that I'm going to buy two!

c I'm .... that you like your present.

d Are you ready for the football game? The children are .... to start!

e Why did I read that book? It was .... that I cried all night!

f This walk is .... I didn't know that the countryside here is ....

3 Match the beginnings, middles and endings of the sentences.

a The film was — so difficult that — I ate three slices!

b That cake was • so good that • he cancelled it.

c The Biology exam was — so busy that — I watched it twice.

d I'm sorry I can't help you this morning. I'm — so poor that — I don't have any free time.

so delicious that

e The song became — so anxious that — everyone was singing it.

f When he thought about the trip, he became — so popular that — I couldn't finish it.

they could only afford soup for dinner.

g The family was

4 Complete the sentences. Use *such* + an adjective and a noun from each box.

> boring difficult ridiculous
> spicy strong ~~successful~~

> man meal opera
> question story ~~team~~

a They were ___such a successful team___ that they easily won the championship.

b It was .... that I fell asleep after an hour! The story and the music were so dull!

c He was .... that he could pull a truck 300 metres.

d The teacher asked .... Nobody in the class could answer it.

e It was .... that no one could eat it.

f He told me .... I didn't believe a word of it.

I can ...

Say that there is more of something than is good

too

The room isn't ready! The VIPs will be here in five minutes! Hurry!

Is it **too late** to reprint all the name labels?

Sorry, I'm **too busy** to talk to you now ...

The security check is taking **too long**.

The water! There's far **too little**.

And there are **too few** glasses.

The lights are **too bright** and the room's **too hot**.

There are **too many people** and there's **too much noise**.

It's **too late** to change everything!

---

too + adjective
= there is more of something than is good (or more than is necessary, or more than I wanted or expected)

It's too hot. = **It is hotter than is good.**
There are too many people. = **There are more people than is good.**

---

too many + countable / *too much* + uncountable / *too few* + countable / *too little* + uncountable

too many people   *too much noise*   *too few glasses*   *too little water*

We can also use *too* + adverb.

The reporters are talking too loudly. = **more loudly than is good.**

Use **too + adjective + to (verb)** to explain the result of something being too hot / cold / noisy / late, etc.

I'm very <u>tired</u>. So I can't <u>go to</u> the dance.

I'm too <u>tired</u> to <u>go to</u> the dance.

It's very <u>late</u>. I can't <u>change</u> everything.

It's too <u>late</u> to <u>change</u> everything.

The film was very frightening. We couldn't watch it.

The film was too frightening to watch.

 ~~*The film was too frightening to watch it.*~~ ✗

1 Freddy is saying why he can't do some things. What are his excuses? Use *too* + an adjective from the box.

dark   expensive   far   ~~late~~
narrow   poor   tired

a

I can't do it. It's .... *too late.*

b

I can't drive there. It's ....

c

I can't buy that. It's ....

I can't buy that. I'm much ....

d

Riga 2760 km

I can't drive there. It's ....

e

I can't finish the work. I'm ....

f

I can't work in this room. It's much ....

2 Describe what you can see in each picture. Use *too many*, *too much*, *too few*, *too little* and a noun from the box.

cakes   noise   passengers   ~~plates~~
seats   time   work

a

too many plates ....

b

....

c

....

d

One minute!

....

e

....

f

342

....

g

....

3 Join the two sentences using *too*.

a These instructions are very complicated. I can't understand them.
These instructions are too complicated to understand.

b They were very lazy. They didn't finish the work.

....

c This river is very dangerous. We can't swim in it.

....

d The owner is very ill. He can't see you.

....

e Martin is very shy. He can't talk to Jane.

....

f I'm very embarrassed. I can't say what I did.

....

 **I can ...**

Say that there is less of something than is good

enough

I'm bored! Let's go out!

I've only got $7. It's **not enough**.

We can go to the second-hand shops and find some cheap clothes.

I've got **enough clothes** for this term. I don't need any more.

OK ... let's go for a run round the park!

Sorry! You're **not fit enough** to run round the park!

Right! Let's play a word game.

I'm **not clever enough**!

We could invite all our friends round here for a meal.

We haven**'t** got **enough food**. There are**n't enough plates** for them.

OK! That's **enough**! I've had **enough** of your excuses! See you later! Bye!

---

not enough = there is less of something than is good (or less than is necessary, or less than I wanted or expected)

***not enough* + noun**

We haven't got enough food.
There aren't enough plates.

We can leave out the noun if the meaning is clear.

It's not enough (money).

not* + adjective + *enough

I'm not clever enough.
You're not fit enough.

In the positive, **enough** = as much as you need.

I've got enough (clothes).

Thanks. I've had enough (food).

... enough ... to do something

You're not fit enough to run round the park!

Have we got enough potatoes to make French fries?

... enough ... for something / someone

I've got enough clothes for this term.

There aren't enough plates for them.

That's enough!
= I don't want to do this any more.

I've had enough of your excuses.
= I am annoyed and bored with your excuses, and don't want to listen any more.

1 Say what people didn't have enough of. Use ideas from the pictures. (Different answers are possible.)

a
Lots of people came to the meeting. We *didn't have enough chairs.*

b
Selin wanted to buy the guitar, but she ....

c
The chef was making a large curry when he realised that he ....

d
I needed to finish the application before midday, but I ....

e
William asked Carol to give him a lift to Manchester, but she ....

f
Leo wanted to write an imaginative story, but he ....

2 Complete Eddie's sentences to say why he thinks some things are impossible.

~~brave~~   confident   hot
intelligent   rich   tall   well

a I can't do that bungee jump! I'm ..*not brave enough.*

b I don't understand nuclear science. I'm ....

c I can't sunbathe today. It's ....

d My seven-year-old daughter is only 1.2 metres. She can't go on the rollercoaster because she's ....

e She doesn't want to sing a song in the end of term show. She's ....

f I can't afford flying lessons. I'm ....

g Terry has a bad cold. He's .... to go to work.

3 ABOUT YOU

Complete the sentences so that they are true for you.

a I'm not ...*old*... enough ..*to get married.*

b I'm not .... enough ....

c I've got enough .... for ....

d I haven't got enough .... to ....

e I've had enough of ....

Adjective + preposition collocations (1)

I'm learning Japanese!

Really! Why?

Well … I'm quite **curious about** life in Japan. And I'm **interested in** Japanese culture.

Do you like your lessons?

Yes. I'm very **enthusiastic about** them. I'm **delighted with** my teacher and I'm really **satisfied with** her classes.

She said she's fairly **impressed with** my pronunciation!

I'm **hopeful about** my exam. I think I'm **capable of** good results.

I'm very **serious about** my studies. I'm **keen on** learning more.

I'm **excited about** going to Kyoto next summer.

curious			satisfied			interested	in
enthusiastic			impressed	with		keen	on
excited	about		delighted			capable	of
hopeful						surprised	by / at
serious						shocked	

Adjective + preposition can be followed by:

a noun phrase:
I'm excited about the holiday.

verb + -ing:
I'm excited about going on holiday.

1 Complete the sentences with *about, with, in, on, of* or *by*.

a This nature programme is so boring. I'm not really interested __in__ fish!

b The tourists were all surprised _____ the hotel manager's rudeness.

c Are you curious _____ your test results?

d Aghh! I can't do this. I'm not capable _____ remembering all this vocabulary!

e Buenos Aires was great and I was very impressed _____ the restaurants! Wow!

f Don't be shocked _____ my news! I've got married!

g Matt's very keen _____ stamp collecting – but I think it's boring.

h I think Suzanne's really serious _____ working in Africa.

i Dave's hopeful _____ getting an A grade for his essay.

j I'm delighted _____ my birthday presents. Thank you all!

2 <u>Underline</u> the correct answer in each sentence.

Angelina Pepper (Secret Agent XX5) sat at the café table opposite Enemy Agent DZ2. Her envelope full of cash was on the table in front of them. She stared into his eyes.

a 'I'm not <u>satisfied with</u> / *capable of* your promise,' she told the enemy agent.

b 'If you are *delighted with* / *serious about* it, give me the secrets now!' she said.

c He laughed. Angelina was very *surprised by* / *keen on* his reaction.

d 'I'm *satisfied with* / *shocked by* your low offer,' he replied. 'I need a lot more money.'

e 'Are you *delighted with* / *interested in* discussing this more?' he asked.

f 'OK,' said Angelina. 'But I'm not *hopeful about* / *capable of* the result.'

g 'I'm *curious about* / *keen on* your instructions,' said DZ2. 'What did your boss tell you about me?'

h 'He warned me that you are *enthusiastic about* / *capable of* anything,' said Angelina.

i 'He's right,' replied DZ2. 'So, please don't be *shocked by* / *serious about* my behaviour.'

j DZ2 grabbed the envelope of money from the table, pulled out his gun and ran out of the café. 'Goodnight, Miss Pepper,' he shouted. 'I'm very *hopeful about* / *satisfied with* our meeting.'

k Angelina pulled out her phone. 'Yes,' she said to her boss. 'He did exactly what we wanted. Everything went well. I am *delighted with* / *curious about* the result. He took the envelope with the computer chip in it. Now we can find his whole gang!'

3 *ABOUT* YOU

Complete the sentences so that they are true for you.

a I was delighted *with my exam results.*

b I'm quite hopeful _____

c I'm usually enthusiastic _____

d I'm not very keen _____

e I was really shocked _____

f My family were very impressed _____

Describe people's characters

Adjective + preposition collocations (2)

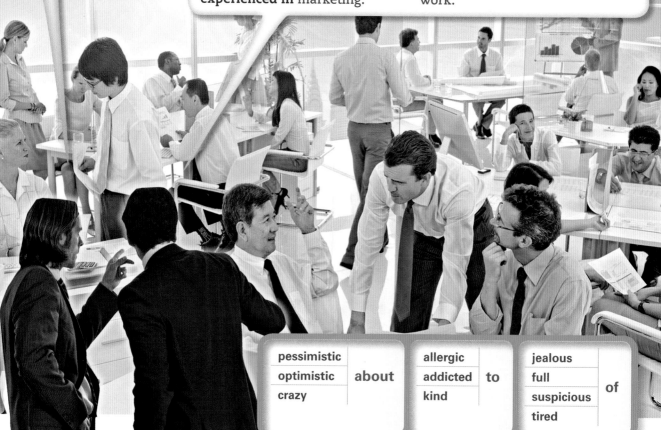

I want to promote one person to Senior Manager. What do you know about them, Mike?

Well …
Fiona's **brilliant at** sales and she's **crazy about** new technology.
Lorna's **famous for** her great presentations and she's very **experienced in** marketing.

Emma's really **good at** languages. Sam's **suspicious of** everyone and he's **addicted to** coffee – he drinks it all the time.
Sarah shouldn't be a Senior Manager. She's **allergic to** hard work.

pessimistic		allergic		jealous	
optimistic	about	addicted	to	full	of
crazy		kind		suspicious	
				tired	

good		experienced	in
brilliant		famous	for
terrible	at		
slow			

1 Complete the sentences with *about*, *to*, *of*, *at*, *in* or *for*.

a I did badly in the oral exam, and I'm pessimistic __about__ the written paper.

b She was always very jealous .... her brother.

c I know I'm boasting, but I'm brilliant .... cooking Indian food.

d Poor Neil! He's addicted .... video games.

e Don't ask me to help! I'm terrible .... remembering names.

f OH! LOOK! He's on TV now! I'm crazy .... him!

g I'm so sorry. I can't eat prawns. I'm allergic .... them.

h Gary said he didn't take her file, but June is still suspicious .... him.

i She's famous .... her voice – she sings beautifully.

j He's tired .... working such long hours.

2 **ABOUT** YOU

Complete the sentences so that they are true for you.

a I'm optimistic *about the future.* ....

b I'm brilliant ....

c I'm tired ....

d I'm famous ....

e I'm terrible ....

f I'm crazy ....

More practice

Adjective + preposition collocations (3)

So ... tell me how you feel ...

I'm so **bored with** housework ...
I'm **fed up with** cleaning and ironing ...
but I'm **proud of** my cooking!

I feel **angry with** my husband.
I'm **angry about** his laziness.
I'm quite **disappointed with** him.
I'm **worried about** our relationship.

I'm really **nervous about** my driving test.

I'm **afraid of** lifts. I'm **frightened of** spiders.

But ... I'm **excited about** my new job.

bored			proud			worried		
pleased	**with**		fond			happy		
fed up			afraid	**of**		amazed		**about**
			frightened			nervous		
			terrified			excited		

angry		He's terribly angry with his boss.	angry	**about ...** something	He's extremely angry about the pay cut.
disappointed	**with ...** a person	Olga's disappointed with herself.	upset		Terry's upset about the bad weather.
upset		Frank's upset with Peggy.	disappointed	**about or with** something	I'm so disappointed about the cancellation.

1 Complete the sentences with *with*, *of* or *about*.

a I'm very worried ...*about*... Lenny. He's behaving strangely.

b Caroline was very excited .... the play.

c I'm so disappointed .... version 3 of this software. It's worse than version 2!

d Take that costume off! Delia is really frightened .... clowns.

e Can we go home? I'm so bored .... this party.

f I'm fed up .... your bad behaviour!

g The children are both very fond .... animals.

h Are you nervous .... your dentist's appointment?

i I'm very angry .... Paul. He promised to give me a lift, but he forgot!

j I'm very angry .... the exam results.

2 Use the words in brackets to describe how Bo felt.

a Bo won a new car in a competition. (amazed / prize)
He was amazed about his prize.

b Bo took his driving test. (nervous / test)

c He failed the driving test. (disappointed / result)

d Three months later, he tried again. This time, he passed his test. (happy / result)

e He couldn't wait to get on the road. (excited / driving)

f The next day, someone stole his car. (angry / theft)

More practice

Are you **happy with** your son's teacher?

Oh, yes! She's wonderful. She's so **nice to** the children. So **kind to** them. She's **gentle with** the young ones ... ... and very **friendly to** them. Oh ... and she was so **generous to** everyone last week! She gave them all chocolates!

That was **kind of** her!

I've noticed that the children are always **polite to** her.

What about the head teacher?

Oh dear! We don't like him very much! He seems quite **unkind** and **unfriendly to** the children. He's sometimes **rude to** parents, too!

What's the head teacher's name?

Oh, I've forgotten! How **silly of** me.

Hang on ... it's the same name as the school, isn't it?

St Hugh's! That was **clever of** you!

I/You/He/She/We/They	am/is/are was/were	kind		other people.
		unkind		
		nice		
		friendly		
		unfriendly		
		helpful	to	
		unhelpful		
		polite		
		rude		
		generous		
		cruel		
		gentle	with	

It is/was	kind	of	her	to do something.
	helpful			
	generous			

That is/was	kind	of	me/you/him/her/us/them.
	unkind		
	nice		
	friendly		
	unfriendly		
	helpful		
	unhelpful		
	polite		
	rude		
	generous		
	cruel		
	smart		
	clever		
	naughty		
	thoughtful		
	sensible		
	silly		
	stupid		

⚠️ **Nice** usually means 'kind', 'enjoyable' or 'pleasant', but the meaning is very general. Some people use the word too much – and some people hate it when everything is called 'nice'! We can make our conversation and stories more precise and more interesting by choosing different adjectives.

She was nice. → *She was friendly.* *It was a nice hotel.* → *It was a comfortable, attractive hotel.*

What a nice dress! → *What a beautiful dress!* *Be nice to him.* → *Be polite and helpful to him.*

1 Complete the sentences with *to* or *of*.

a The hotel manager was very unhelpful *to* the tourists who arrived late.

b She stuck her tongue out at me! That's very rude .... her.

c Don't worry about Matilda! She's rude .... everyone!

d Oh! They've left their toys all over the floor! That's naughty .... them!

e The old station master was kind .... the boys and answered all their questions.

f She told me to find another seat! I thought that was really unhelpful .... her.

g It was generous .... Marie to help the drama club so much.

h Caitlin was generous .... the children.

2 In each sentence, think of three more interesting adjectives you could use instead of *nice*. Remember that you may need to change *a/an* as well. (Many different answers are possible.)

a That was a nice story.

→ *an exciting story / a boring story / a thrilling story*

b Thank you! That was a nice meal!

→ ....

c Wow! There's a nice view from your balcony.

→ ....

d What a nice museum!

→ ....

e This is a really nice song!

→ ....

f The optician was nice.

→ ....

g Come in! The swimming pool is nice!

→ ....

h It's a nice day. Let's have a picnic!

→ ....

Say how I travelled and where I stayed

Where did you go?

We **went on holiday** to Germany this year. We **travelled by train from** London **to** Berlin – then **by underground** to our hotel.

I **went on a business trip** to Sofia last month. I **stayed in an old hotel** right **in the centre of** town. I was in a tiny room **at the back** of the building!

We **went on an amazing trip** all over Europe. We **went by ferry** and **by train** and **coach**.

On their first day in Peru, Susie and George **went on a guided tour** of Lima. Then they **went by road** to Machu Picchu.

We **stayed in a small farmhouse** in the countryside. It was really hot **in the sun** ... so we **sat in the shade** all day.

What you did

went	on	holiday
		a guided tour
		a trip / a business trip

How you travelled

went	by	land
		road
		rail
		air
		sea

The transport you used

went	by	bus / minibus / (long-distance) coach
		(intercity / express / high-speed) train
		ship / boat / ferry
		car / taxi / cab
		bicycle / bike / motorbike
		plane
	on	foot
		the 10 o'clock bus / an express train
	in	Martha's car / my car / a company car / an ambulance

Where you went

went	to	Germany/Dresden
	from	London to Berlin
stayed	in	São Paulo
		a great hotel
		the centre of town
		the countryside
	on	the twenty-third floor
		a small ship
sat	in	the sun
		the shade
had a room	at	the front / back

⚠️ *by car / by taxi / by cab* **but** *in a car / in my car / in John's car / in a yellow cab*

by train / by high-speed train **but** *on a train / on the 10 o'clock train / on a high-speed train*

1 Complete the sentences using *by*, *on* or *in* and a word from the box.

> air   ambulance   bike   ~~bus~~   ferry
> foot   high-speed train   my car

a

She went ..*by bus.*..

b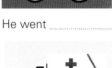

He went ....

c

She went ....
....

d

They took her to the hospital ....

e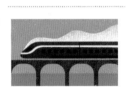

We all went ....

f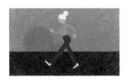

Trudie went from Ghent to Brussels ....

g

They crossed the lake ....

h

I usually travel to Geneva ....

2 Complete the sentences with *by*, *at*, *to*, *in* or *on*.

a Last time we visited Bratislava we stayed ..*in*.. the town centre.

b Teresa went .... a three-day trip to Singapore.

c It's a beautiful day. Let's sit .... the shade.

d They gave me a very cold room .... the back of the building.

e I love staying .... the countryside.

f I usually travel around China .... plane, but on this trip I'm going everywhere .... train.

g She took me .... a wonderful guided tour of Bologna.

3 *ABOUT* **YOU**

Describe three journeys (long or short) that you took recently.

a *We went on a business trip to Saudi Arabia. We stayed in Kamal's flat in the centre of Riyadh.*

b ....
....

c ....
....

Collocations: noun + **for** and noun + **of**

for

I'm a manager at a large supermarket. In a normal day I have a thousand little problems! When the shop is busy ... we all have to help.

of

Excuse me! Where can I find eggs?

Aisle 17. Look up. Can you see a big **picture of** an egg? And a **photo of** 'Eggy Man'?

What's the **reason for** this? There's flour all over the floor!

Can you tell me what crème fraiche is?

Well ... It's a **sort of** sour cream.

Who has **responsibility for** the frozen food department today?

Why don't you sell goat's milk?

There are only two **boxes of** chocolate cookies on this shelf! Why?

The **rest of** them are in the warehouse.

I'm sorry. There's no **room for** it.

What are the **advantages of** working here? Well ... a wide **variety of** people shop here, so I meet lots of different **types of** people.

Can you talk to a customer who is interested in working here?

I'm sorry, I don't have **time for** that.

I don't like this job. There's a total **lack of** support. I don't think our manager sees the **value of** happy staff! That's the main **cause of** all our problems!

Noun + *for*

time		
responsibility		
a reason		
an explanation	**for**	something
a demand		
room		
an application		
respect		someone

If an item is a *sort of* something, it is very similar to something else, but not exactly the same.

The rest (of them) means the ones that are left.

One of the cats is light-coloured, and the rest are darker.

Noun + *of*

a result			a photo		
a lack			a picture		
a sort			a jpeg		
the rest	**of**	something	a cartoon		
the value			a painting		
the cause			a drawing	**of**	something / someone
a variety			a portrait		
a type			a sketch		
			an illustration		
an advantage	**of**	(doing) something	a poster		
a disadvantage			an animation		

a box		
a case	**of**	something
a packet		

1 Complete the sentences with *for* or *of*.

a When I get home, I'm going to write an application *for* that job in Hong Kong.

b Briony drew a fantastic sketch .... her sister.

c The car wouldn't start. Robert had no idea what the cause .... the problem was.

d Sorry! The seminar is full. There's no room .... any more people.

e Are you going to the shop? Could you get me a packet .... biscuits, please?

f I can see one DVD on the shelf – but where are the rest .... them?

g My boss gave me responsibility .... preparing the photocopies.

h A donkey is a sort .... horse.

2 Complete the sentences with one word from the box and *for* or *of*.

> disadvantages   jpeg   ~~lack~~   reason   respect   time   types

a This is a dreadful instruction book. There's a serious ....*lack of*.... information about how the toy works.

b Did you know? There are over 150,000 different .... moth!

c Your plane landed at the wrong airport! What was the .... that?

d I've just downloaded a hilarious .... a kitten on top of a computer printer!

e What are the .... this new tax?

f This traffic jam is so slow! We're late already. We don't have .... more delays.

g Be polite and listen to George! You have to show .... other people's ideas.

3 Complete the second sentence so that it means the same as the first.

a He wrote a job application.
He wrote an application *for a job.*

b Holbein painted the king's portrait.
Holbein painted a portrait ....

c Patsy hasn't heard her exam results yet.
Patsy hasn't heard the results ....

d Her accident was caused by rain.
Rain was the cause ....

e Shane has got spare parts in a box.
Shane has got a box ....

f Mrs Andrews explained her son's strange behaviour.
Mrs Andrews gave an explanation ....

More practice

I can ...

Talk about working with difficult people

Collocations: noun + **with**

You wanted to see me, sir?

Ah, Tom. Thank you for coming. I wanted to have a little **chat with** you. I heard that you had an **argument with** Susanna. Is that true?

Um. Yes, sir. Actually, I've had some serious **disagreements with** her over the last month or two.

Do you have a **problem with** her?

Well ... I don't have a good **relationship with** her. I can't even start a **conversation with** her. She just gets angry. Whenever I try to **do business with** a new client, she always says I do it badly. So, yes ... I have real **trouble with** her – she's always so critical.

OK. I think we need a **meeting with** you and her together. We need to spend a little **time with** each other ... all in the same room ...

have	a meeting	with	someone
	a chat		
	a conversation		
	a discussion		
	an argument		
	a disagreement		
	a problem		
	trouble		
	a good / bad relationship		
	a battle		
do	business		
spend	time		

If you *have a battle* with someone, it means you argue (not fight!).

1 Match the questions with the responses.

a Who did you have your meeting with?
b Have you had a chat with Mary about the new catalogue yet?
c Do you think we need to do more business with Japan?
d Did you have a good relationship with your parents?
e Do you like spending time with her?

1 Yes. It's a very big market.
2 No. They always got angry with me.
3 All the senior management team.
4 Definitely. She's great fun!
5 Yes, we bumped into each other this morning.

2 Write the word *with* in the correct place in each sentence.

a The children had a terrible argument *with* their grandma.

b Sean has never had a good relationship his father.

c Are the boys having any problems their new teacher?

d Did I have a conversation about the new computers you yesterday? I can't remember.

e Every summer we spend time in the countryside our children.

3 ABOUT YOU

Complete the sentences so that they are true for you.

a I had a difficult meeting .with.my.boss.last.Wednesday.
b I have a really good relationship ....
c I never have arguments ....
d I often have long conversations ....
e I like to spend my free time ....

I can ... Talk about what I do online

Verb + preposition collocations

Oh wow! That's amazing news about Freddy and Jill. I'm going to **blog about** it!

I was first! I've already **tweeted about** it!

I **made friends with** three great new people on Facebook last night.

Look! Mandy's **shared** some photos of the picnic **with** us.

My phone's so slow! You have to **wait for** ages!

I **searched for** his company, but I couldn't find his email address.

No problem! **Look through** the company web pages and **look for** his name. **Look at** the picture to check if it's the right person. Then **look up** his email address!

search / wait / pay	for	something / someone

blog / tweet	about	something / someone

| share | (something) | with |
| make | friends | |

	at		= move your eyes so that you can see something
look	for	something / someone	= try to find something or someone
	up		= find information in a book, list, website, etc.
	through	something	= quickly look at a number of pages in a website (or book or magazine) (perhaps because you want to find something)

These verbs do not usually need a preposition:
join, post, email, text, edit, upload, download

I joined Ø a new forum / website / club, etc.
I emailed Ø him.
(BUT … **he emailed something <u>to</u> me** e.g. *Peter emailed the contract to me.*)
She texted Ø me.
(BUT … **she texted something <u>to</u> me** e.g. *Sarah texted Tom's phone number to me.*)
I posted Ø a message.
Mike edited Ø his profile.
We uploaded Ø some photos.
She downloaded Ø the new album.

1 Complete the sentences with *for, about, through* or *with*.

a Gabrielle searched online __for__ the office address.
b Check your messages! I've just shared some amazing pictures of giraffes _____ you!
c My phone is very slow! I'm still waiting _____ your pictures to download!
d When I got to the checkout, I paid _____ the e-books with my credit card.
e I've just blogged _____ that terrible café! We should complain!
f I've never met Barry, but I feel I know him quite well! He tweets _____ everything he does!
g Could you look _____ these web pages, please, and check if there are any spelling mistakes? Thanks!
h I love this new website! I've made friends _____ so many new people!

2 Some of the sentences have a mistake. If the sentence is good, write ✓. If it is wrong, write ✗ and cross out one incorrect word.

a I emailed my brother about his passport problems. ✓
b Last night, Tony edited ~~about~~ his Facebook profile. ✗
c I spent all afternoon uploading with my holiday photos. _____
d Oh, Kelly! Tell me that you didn't *really* join to the new BestFace forum! _____
e Did you make friends with those new members? _____
f I've looked everywhere for my password – but I can't find it! _____
g Hey, everyone. I've just posted up a new message on my blog. _____
h Ted spent five minutes looking at the picture, but he couldn't find me in it! _____
i Could you email the director's contact details to me, please? _____

REVIEW UNIT
There's a lot more in *Visual Grammar A2*

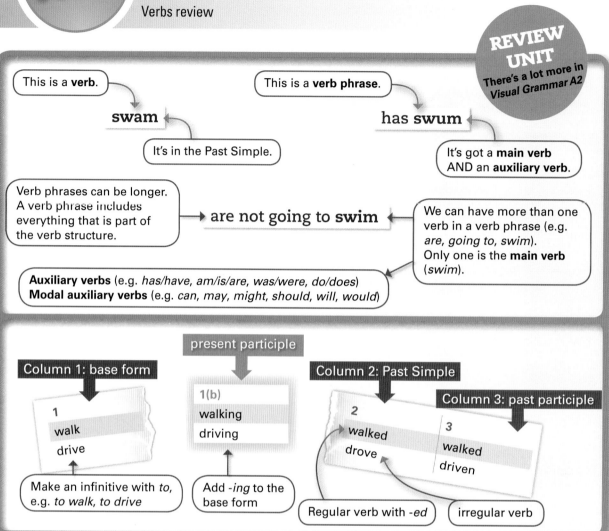

This is a **verb**.

swam

It's in the Past Simple.

This is a **verb phrase**.

has **swum**

It's got a **main verb** AND an **auxiliary verb**.

Verb phrases can be longer. A verb phrase includes everything that is part of the verb structure.

→ are not going to **swim** ←

We can have more than one verb in a verb phrase (e.g. *are, going to, swim*). Only one is the **main verb** (*swim*).

Auxiliary verbs (e.g. *has/have, am/is/are, was/were, do/does*)
Modal auxiliary verbs (e.g. *can, may, might, should, will, would*)

present participle

Column 1: base form

1
walk
drive

Make an infinitive with *to*, e.g. *to walk, to drive*

1(b)
walking
driving

Add *-ing* to the base form

Column 2: Past Simple

Column 3: past participle

2
walked
drove

3
walked
driven

Regular verb with *-ed*

irregular verb

---

1 Underline the verb phrases.

  a I'll walk to the station.
  b The children are going to eat lunch in the garden.
  c She's been to New Delhi.
  d What are you going to do about it?
  e The soldiers were driving too fast.
  f Trudie's answering the phone right now.

2 Match the main verbs or verb phrases a–h with the correct name 1–8.

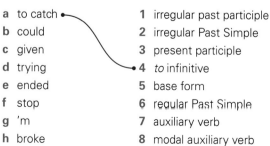

  a to catch   **1** irregular past participle
  b could   **2** irregular Past Simple
  c given   **3** present participle
  d trying   **4** *to* infinitive
  e ended   **5** base form
  f stop   **6** regular Past Simple
  g 'm   **7** auxiliary verb
  h broke   **8** modal auxiliary verb

3 Complete the table *without* looking at a verb table.

1	2	3
see	saw	seen
watch	_____ a	_____ b
_____ c	_____ d	flown
_____ e	began	_____ f
_____ g	went	_____ h
_____ i	_____ j	drawn
_____ k	fell	_____ l
feel	_____ m	_____ n
catch	_____ o	_____ p
_____ q	chose	_____ r
_____ s	_____ t	forgotten
know	_____ u	_____ v
mean	_____ w	_____ x
_____ y	hurt	_____ z

More practice

Present Progressive for changing situations

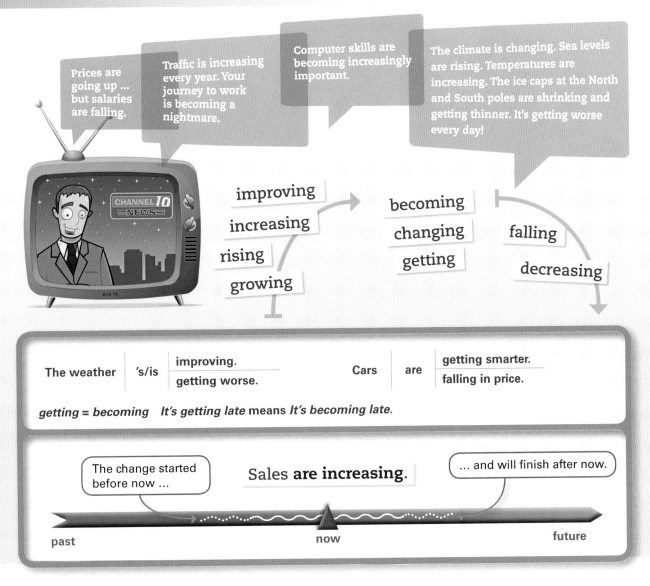

Prices are going up ... but salaries are falling.

Traffic is increasing every year. Your journey to work is becoming a nightmare.

Computer skills are becoming increasingly important.

The climate is changing. Sea levels are rising. Temperatures are increasing. The ice caps at the North and South poles are shrinking and getting thinner. It's getting worse every day!

improving
increasing
rising
growing

becoming
changing
getting

falling
decreasing

| The weather | 's/is | improving. / getting worse. | | Cars | are | getting smarter. / falling in price. |

getting = becoming   *It's getting late* means *It's becoming late*.

The change started before now ...

Sales are increasing.

... and will finish after now.

past — now — future

---

1 Write the verbs in brackets in the Present Progressive.

Our town _is growing_ ª (grow) so fast. I think it _____ ᵇ (get) bigger all the time. The local newspaper says that it _____ ᶜ (become) an important business centre. I don't know about that – but certainly the company where I work _____ ᵈ (expand)!

And look out of this window! Can you see? They _____ ᵉ (build) a new shopping mall over there. The noise _____ ᶠ (get) louder every day!

2 Use the words to make sentences about things that are changing.

a Prices / go up
Prices are going up.

b The internet / change all the time

c My English marks / get better

d The cost of living / increase

e Mobile phone charges / rise again

f The population / get older

More practice

I can ... **Use present tenses**

Present Simple and Present Progressive review

Present Simple	She runs. → Does she run? → She doesn't run.
Present Progressive	She's running. (= She is running) → Is she running? → She isn't running.

Are present tenses always about the present? No!

One tense	can refer to	different times.
One time	can be talked about using	different tenses.

Present Simple is used for:

- things that are always true (past, present and future)

  Deserts become very cold at night.

- repeated events, habits and routines (past, present and future)

  John travels to London every morning.

- past events in jokes and anecdotes

  A bear walks into a café ...

- states now and around now

  I love this food.

  Some verbs (e.g. *believe, like, have, feel, want, love*) don't describe an action. They describe a state – i.e. a situation that lasts for some time. They are called **stative verbs**. We usually use stative verbs in simple (not progressive) tenses.

  I'm liking him. ✗ → *I like him.* ✓

Present Progressive is used for:

- things happening now and right around now

  She's laughing.

  I'm cooking breakfast for everyone.

- longer, temporary events, starting in the past and going into the future

  We're studying in Paris.

- changing situations

  The population is growing older.

- planned events in the future

  I'm seeing my favourite band tonight (**see unit 49**).

1 Complete the sentences with the words in the box.

> am   are   ask   asking   does   don't
> have   having   ~~is~~   think   thinking

a The Prime Minister ____is____ speaking about Europe.

b The women .... leaving in a few minutes.

c I .... like chocolate, but I love ginger biscuits!

d Where .... your sister live?

e Two Englishmen walk into a café, and .... the waiter for one ice cream and two spoons.

f Are you studying in Berlin or do you .... a job?

g Do you really .... aliens are real?

h .... I late for our meeting?

i Is that surfer .... trouble with her board?

j I'm not .... for special treatment! I just want a menu!

k I'm .... of moving to another country.

2 For each sentence
1 name the <u>underlined</u> tense
2 say if it refers to past, present or future.

a We<u>'re driving</u> home at 10 o'clock.
   1 *Present Progressive*   2 *future – later today*

b I<u>'m leaving</u> at the end of the month.
   1 ....   2 ....

c My birthday <u>is</u> on a Saturday this year.
   1 ....   2 ....

d Sandra<u>'s working</u> in the small office at the end of the corridor.
   1 ....   2 ....

e When you <u>arrive</u>, get a taxi at the station.
   1 ....   2 ....

f In winter, the lake <u>freezes</u>.
   1 ....   2 ....

3 Complete the sentences with the verb in brackets in the named tense.

a Susie *...'s preparing...* a new folder of information for the meeting.
(prepare – Present Progressive)

b Pete .... a cheese sandwich for lunch!
(want – Present Simple)

c The engineers .... around midday.
(arrive – Present Progressive)

d Lena .... to Katowice every Friday.
(go – Present Simple)

e Tim .... the report.
(read – Present Progressive)

f We .... on this project for another two months. (work – Present Progressive)

g Shaun .... in ghosts!
(not believe – Present Simple)

4 Use the verbs in brackets to complete the sentences. Decide whether to use the Present Simple or the Present Progressive.

a I'll come in five minutes! I *...'m finishing...* my work. (finish)

b I .... work at 6.00 pm on Fridays. (finish)

c Ben .... his mind all the time! (change)

d Quick! The film ....! (start)

e Maggy .... romantic movies! (not like)

f In the evening, Karen .... at a clothing factory. (work)

g This month, Ronnie .... in a primary school. (work)

h Josie .... at a medical conference tomorrow afternoon. (speak)

i Josie .... three languages: English, Vietnamese and Cantonese. (speak)

j Our three-year-old, Nick, ... all the time, day and night! (talk)

k I can't understand what Nick .... about. (talk)

I can ... Talk about events in the past

Past Simple, Past Progressive, Present Perfect Simple review

REVIEW UNIT
There's a lot more in *Visual Grammar A2*

Past Simple	She ran → Did she run? → She didn't run
Past Progressive	She was running → Was she running? → She wasn't running
Present Perfect Simple	She's run (= She has run) → Has she run? → She hasn't run

She bought a coat.
Past Simple — An action at a time in the past

They lived in Denver.
Past Simple — A longer event in the past

The children usually played 'shops' every weekend.
Past Simple — A repeated past habit

They were working last night.
Past Progressive — An event that was in progress at a time in the past

While I was checking the passengers, Sinead was landing the plane.
Past Progressive & Past Progressive — Two events that were happening at the same time

Mike was eating his lunch when the police arrived.
Past Progressive & Past Simple — A past event interrupted by another

She met him while she was visiting the zoo.
Past Simple & Past Progressive — Something that happened during another event

He's just arrived.
Present Perfect — An action immediately before now

We've all seen that film.
Present Perfect — An experience before now (exactly when it happened is not important)

They've washed the floor.
Present Perfect — A past action that has a result now (e.g. the floor is now clean)

1 Name the tense(s) used in each sentence.

  a Tony took Alison to the cinema. _Past Simple_

  b Have you eaten my sandwich?

  c What were the kids doing all afternoon?

  d Did you take them to the zoo?

  e I wasn't playing with your keyboard! Honest!

  f Graham's just given this to me.

  g Was it working?

  h Harry came to see her every weekend.

  i They didn't feel ill, but they were feeling cold.

  j When we arrived, our teacher stopped talking and stared at us!

  k I was walking past your house when I heard a loud noise.

  l While you were washing the dishes, Fred was watching TV.

  m The whole class has seen that film.

  n In those days, we lived in Greece. We met at university. We were both studying Maths.

2 Complete Ted's sentences and Jan's questions with the verb in brackets in the named tense.

  a Ted: Michael _was having_ lunch when I saw him. (have – Past Progressive)

   Jan: What _was he eating_ ? (eat – Past Progressive)

  b Ted: I .... you before! (tell – Present Perfect)

   Jan: What .... me? (tell – Past Simple)

  c Ted: They .... to Cuba. (go – Present Perfect)

   Jan: When .... ? (go – Past Simple)

  d Ted: Those students .... a terrible noise all evening! (make – Past Simple)

   Jan: What .... ? (do – Past Progressive)

  e Ted: They .... a long distance bus. (catch – Past Simple)

   Jan: Which bus .... ? (catch – Past Simple)

  f Ted: Oh no! They .... it. (break – Present Perfect)

   Jan: What .... ? (break – Present Perfect)

  g Ted: Look! I .... this amazing sports car! (buy – Past Simple)

   Jan: Wow! .... a fast car before? (drive – Present Perfect)

  h Ted: Ow! Your stupid dog .... my leg! (bite – Present Perfect)

   Jan: .... him? (annoy – Past Simple)

3 Write the verb in brackets in the correct tense (Past Simple, Past Progressive or Present Perfect). (Different answers may be possible.)

  a I _gave_ the parcel to your secretary. (give)

  b Cuba? No, I _'ve_ never _been_ there. (go)

  c I don't want to go to the cinema. I .... a few days ago! (go)

  d I checked at 2 o'clock. The children .... quietly in the garden. (play)

  e I first .... my husband while I .... aerobics at the gym. (meet, do)

  f I know you haven't read _Macbeth_, but .... the film? (see)

  g Wow! You went to the ceremony! .... it? (enjoy)

  h We .... in the sea every day when we lived in Australia. (swim)

  i One day, Dan .... about 100m from the shore when he .... a shark! (swim, see)

  j While the students .... the Chemistry exam, the teachers .... the Physics exam. (take, mark)

  k Oh no! Tommy .... just .... his glass of water! (knock over)

I can ...

Give a general idea about when something happened

Time adverbials (for general and indefinite times)

From: Amina
To: Corbin337
Subject: Projector

Hi Conrad,
Yes. Peter has the projector. I gave it to him earlier. OK, I'll ask him later today.

Have you phoned her yet?

No ... no ... no. I'm sorry. I haven't called her yet. I'll do it immediately ... well ... I'll do it soon ... um ... I'll do it later ...

Messages   Edit

Susan still has the financial report.

I don't think we need to cut the price. I'm sure they'll agree to the deal eventually.

I talked to their CEO recently ... Um ... yes, we've met three times previously.

Yes, I've already sent that invoice.

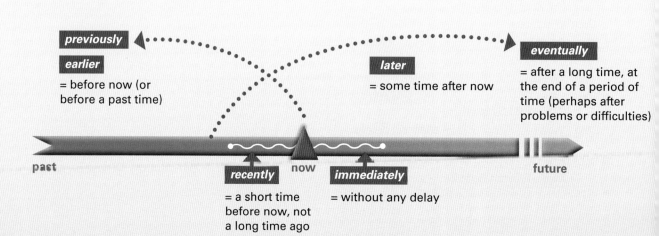

previously

earlier
= before now (or before a past time)

later
= some time after now

eventually
= after a long time, at the end of a period of time (perhaps after problems or difficulties)

past

recently
= a short time before now, not a long time ago

now

immediately
= without any delay

future

yet (in a negative sentence) = not until now
When we use *yet*, we usually expect that the action will happen in the future.

not not not not not not   ??????????

past   now   future

The examiner hasn't arrived yet.
I haven't eaten my lunch yet.

still = true up to now (and possibly into the future)

✓✓✓✓ ✓✓✓✓ ✓✓✓✓ ✓✓   ??????????

past   now   future

Patrick is still working in the garage.
Are you still living in Grange Road?

yet (in a question) = asking if something has happened before now

????????????????????????

past   now   future

Have the singers started yet?
Has order 2257BH arrived yet?

already = before now (or before I expected)

past   now   future

Susie has come to meet the visitors, but they've already left.
I've already read this book.

These three sentences have a very similar meaning:
Have they already finished the exam? / Have they finished the exam already? /
Have they finished the exam yet?

1 Ted asked Ana (his personal assistant) about an important job. <u>Underline</u> the correct word for each of Ana's replies.

a Sorry, I can't do this job now. I'll do it *previously / <u>later</u>*.

b Sorry, I haven't done this job yet. I'll do it *immediately / recently*.

c Yes, I've done the job. I did it *later / earlier*.

d I'm sorry this job is taking so long! I promise I'll do it *eventually / recently*.

e Sorry, I've had so much work *recently / eventually*. There was no free time to work on it.

2 Complete the sentences with *already*, *still* or *yet*.

a I started painting this room at 9 a.m. and I'm ......*still*...... working now – at midnight!

b Let's go to the National Gallery. David has .... been there and he says it's great.

c The children haven't started their lunch ....

d Have you seen Peter ....? He promised he would come in this morning.

e You recommended the film last year, but I .... haven't seen it!

f Has the board meeting .... finished?

g No. The meeting hasn't finished ....

h I think you're right. The managers are .... in the meeting. They haven't left.

3 Reply using the words in brackets. (Different answers are possible.)

a Let's go to see *Alien War 3* at the cinema. (already / see)

No, *I've already seen it!*

b Do your homework now! (do / later)

No, *I'll do it later.*

c Have you finished your homework? (do / earlier)

Yes, ...

d Have you finished your homework? (still / do)

No, ...

e Have you finished your homework? (already / do)

Yes, ...

f Have you been to Zurich? (go / recently)

Yes, ...

g Do you know the Head of Marketing? (meet / previously)

Yes, ...

More practice

Tell an interesting story about my life

Cohesion and coherence: different tenses, direct speech and hesitation devices

Get your listener interested!

You'll never guess what I did yesterday!

What?

Start with a summary of the most important, interesting thing.

I nearly got myself a pet snake!

A snake? Really! Why?

Use a mixture of tenses.

Hesitate using *well, you know, er* and *um*.

Well ... I was visiting Mike in Edinburgh and he, you know, he keeps snakes. So, he showed me all his snakes. He, er, told me about them. They were all a type called, um, corn snakes. They were, you know, they were quite small and very beautiful.

I don't think any snakes are beautiful!

Use *Well, actually* to politely disagree or say you have a different view.

Repeat words to give yourself more time.

Use *anyway* to continue telling your story after an interruption.

Use *I said / he said / she said*, etc. to include the actual words of a conversation.

Well, actually, I thought ... I thought these were gorgeous! Anyway, he said, 'Would you like one?' And I said, 'I've never had any pets. I have no idea how to keep a snake!' And he said, 'Don't worry! They are really easy! They only need food about every ten days.' You know, I almost took one!

But you didn't?

No, I changed my mind when Mike told me what corn snakes eat! His freezer is full of frozen rats!

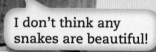

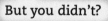

Oh, yuk!

Get your listener interested

Start your story with something to catch your listener's attention.

You'll never guess what I did yesterday!
Do you know who I met this morning?
Can you guess where I went last night?

Summarise

Give a short summary of the most important point of your story at the beginning, so that people know what you are talking about.

I met a pop star last night!

Tenses

The Past Progressive is useful for explaining the background situation before you start the main part of the story.

We were walking into town.
I was living in Seoul.

Most of your story will be in the Past Simple. State things that are always or generally true with the Present Simple.

He keeps snakes.

Hesitating

Hesitate with *er* and *um* to give yourself more time to think. It's better than leaving a long silence!
You can hesitate with *you know* (although some people find this annoying if used too much!)

Leo went, you know, to the supermarket.

Repetition

You can also repeat words to give yourself thinking time.

So we all went, um, we all went to the park.

Well ...

Use *well* to hesitate, especially when you're replying to someone and you want to start telling your story.
Use *well, actually* to politely disagree with what someone has said or to introduce a different view.

I really enjoyed that film.
Well, actually, I thought it was terrible!

Direct speech

Include speech in your stories. Use *I said, He said* or *She said* with the exact words people said. If you write your story, use speech marks.

I said, 'It's a new jacket,' and she said, 'Well, I love it,' and I said, 'I'm so glad.'

1 Look back at the snake story. Name the <u>underlined</u> tenses from the story.

a I nearly <u>got</u> myself a pet snake! ..... *Past Simple*
b I <u>was visiting</u> Mike in Edinburgh. .....
c He <u>keeps</u> snakes. .....
d They <u>were</u> quite small. .....
e I <u>thought</u> these were gorgeous! .....
f I<u>'ve</u> never <u>had</u> any pets. .....
g They <u>are</u> really easy! .....
h I <u>changed</u> my mind. .....
i His freezer <u>is</u> full of frozen rats. .....

2 Complete the story with the verbs in brackets in the named tenses.

In 2010, I .....*was living*[a] (live, Past Progressive) in Riga. One morning I .....[b] (work, Past Progressive) on an important essay. Well, my computer suddenly .....[c] (die, Past Simple). I .....[d] (be, Past Simple) so frightened, you know, that all my work was lost. I .....[e] (call, Past Simple) my friend, Filips. He said, 'What .....you .....[f] (try, Present Perfect question)?' I said, 'Nothing. I .....[g] (panic, Present Progressive)!' He

said, ' .....you .....[h] (make, Present Perfect question) a backup?' I said, 'I .....[i] (know, Present Simple negative) how to!' He .....[j] (mend, Past Simple) my computer and saved my work. He .....[k] (ask, Past Simple) me to have a meal with him that night. I .....[l] (say, Past Simple) yes. Well, anyway, three years later, we .....[m] (get, Past Simple) married.

3 **ABOUT** YOU

Tell a story about something you did in the last three weeks. Try to do these three things:

• Start your story with something to catch your listener's attention.
• Include some *I said / he said / she said* speech.
• Hesitate using *um, er, you know* and *well.*

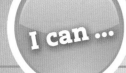

I can ...   Ask how long someone has been doing something

Present Perfect Progressive questions

How long **have** you **been going out with** your boyfriend?

How long **has** she **been writing** poetry?

How long **have** you **been running** marathons?

How long **have** you **been working** at the nuclear power station?

How long **have** they **been watching** TV?

How long **has** she **been driving**?

	has/have		been	+	- ing		
	have	I / you / we / they			waiting		
					working	here	
					living	in Delhi	
					going out	with her	
					doing	that	
How long			been		cooking		?
					running	marathons	
					writing	poetry	
	has	he / she / it			standing	there	
					looking	for work	
					watching	TV	
					playing	tennis	
					driving		

The **Present Perfect Progressive** is used to ask about temporary, unfinished situations that started in the past and continue up to now (and might continue into the future).

Answer with *for* to say the length of time.

for three years
for two hours

Answer with *since* to say when something started.

since two o'clock
since 2013

We can answer with other time expressions, e.g.

all day!
a few minutes
all evening!

We can make other *Wh-* questions with *What* ...? *Where* ...?, etc.

What have you been doing?
Where have you been living?
Who have you been working with?

We can also make questions without *Wh-* question words.

Have you been swimming?
Has she been studying?

Short answers: *Yes, I have. / No, I haven't. / Yes, she has. / No, she hasn't.*, **etc.**

1 Put the words in the correct order to make questions.

a been Paris long have how living you in ?

How long have you been living in Paris?

b working Peter long has how here been ?

c been out how has going Tim with she long ?

d been has doing what she ?

e he staying has where been ?

f been has evening cooking all he ?

g video three have games for playing they hours been ?

h Sarah has working been who with ?

2 Make Present Perfect Progressive questions. Use the words in brackets.

a (How long / he / wait)

How long has he been waiting?

b (Susan / study)

Has Susan been studying?

c (How long / they / watch TV)

d (What / Jenny / cook)

e (Where / he / hide)

f (Jamie / live / Spain)

g (you / play football)

h (How long / those young men / look for work)

3 Use the word pool to make ten different questions. (You can re-use words.)

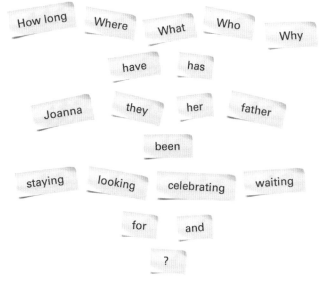

I can ... # Emphasise the length of time of an action

Present Perfect Progressive

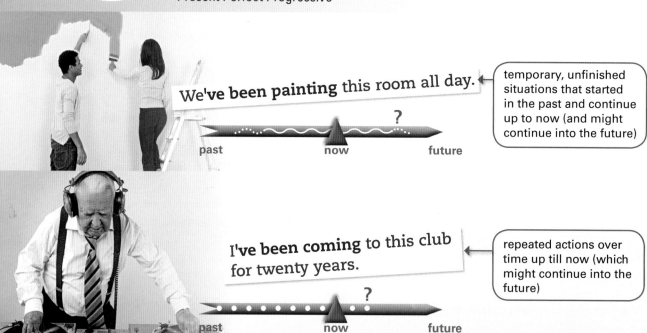

We**'ve been painting** this room all day.

| temporary, unfinished situations that started in the past and continue up to now (and might continue into the future) |

past — now — future — ?

I**'ve been coming** to this club for twenty years.

| repeated actions over time up till now (which might continue into the future) |

past — now — future — ?

Sales **have been rising**.

| changes over time up till now (which might continue into the future) |

past — now — future

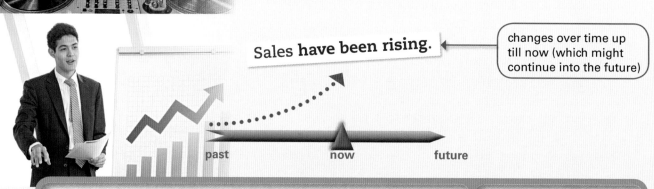

	've / 's		been	+ -ing	
I	've / have			working	here since 2010.
You				making	a good profit.
He / She / It	's / has	(not)	been	increasing	every year.
We	've / have			selling	more products.
They				waiting	a long time.

Often used with time expressions:

for ... (length of time)
since ... (start time)
all day / week / month / year
etc.

We often use this tense when we want to emphasise how long an action takes. For this reason, it is very suitable for:

- telling other people how hard you have been working or how long you have been doing something

  I've been washing dishes all morning!

  The children have been trying so hard, but they can't do their homework.

- complaining and criticising

  I've been waiting for you for ages!

  Ben's been telling me the same thing for twenty years!

  You've been using my iPad for more than an hour!

1 Put the words in the correct order to make sentences.

a July working Cheryl since been in 's Johannesburg

Cheryl's been working in Johannesburg since July.

b talking 've all been night we

....

c you waiting 've morning I for this been since!

....

d very our selling new well hasn't been cheese

....

e working it year 's well all been

....

2 Picture 1 shows when the action started. Picture 2 shows 'now'. Make Present Perfect Progressive sentences using *for*.

a

Fred started waiting outside the cinema at 6 o'clock.
Fred's been waiting outside the cinema for one and a half hours.

b

The baby started playing at 1 o'clock.

....
....

c

TUESDAY 8.00 a.m.   **FRIDAY** 5.00 p.m.

They started working in our street on Tuesday.

....
....

d

JANUARY   **JULY**

Helen started studying at Dance College in January.

....
....

e

The decorators started painting the kitchen wall at 10.15.

....
....

f

1985   2014

DEKKER   DEKKER

Hugh started working at Dekker Furniture in 1985.

....
....

3 Make new Present Perfect Progressive sentences that give the same information as the original sentences. (Different answers may be possible.)

a Jill opened her book at 2 o'clock. Jill's still reading now.

Jill's been reading since 2 o'clock.

b Keith picked up the microphone one hour ago. He is still singing now.

....

c You are wearing the same shirt as yesterday and the day before! You first wore it five days ago!

....

d I asked you yesterday afternoon. I asked you last night. I asked you this morning. I asked you just now.

....

e I thought about the problem seven days ago. I thought about it every day this week. I'm still thinking about it.

....

f We had our first game of cards at midnight. It's 4 a.m. now!

....

g Lara fell asleep at lunchtime. She's still sleeping now.

....

I can ... # Talk about things I did in the past (but not now)

used to

When I was 8

Now!

HAPPY BIRTHDAY!

I **used to** love parties.

I **didn't use to** like pizza.

I **used to** be frightened of clowns.

I **used to** have a superhero costume.

I rarely go to parties now!

Pizza is my favourite food!

I'm not frightened of them any more

I don't have it now.

We use *used to* to talk about things that were true in the past, but not now.

If your friend says *I used to smoke*, she also means ... *but I don't smoke now*.

Used to is always the same. It doesn't change.

I/You/He/She/It/We/They	used to	be a good swimmer.
		like fish and chips.
		wear strange hats.
		say that sport is a waste of time!
		hate rap music.

It's always about the past. There is no present form.
~~We are using to eat chicken and rice every day for lunch.~~ ✗

Make questions with *Did ... use to ...?* or *Wh- + did .. use to ...?*

no *d*!

no *d*!

Did they use to play basketball? Yes, they did./ No, they didn't.

Did Sonia use to go to the 17th District High School? Yes, she did./No, she didn't.

Where did you use to work?

How did you use to go to school?

If your friend asks *Did you use to smoke?* she means *Did you smoke in the past (but not now)?*

no *d*!

Make negatives with *didn't use to.*

The children didn't use to have piano lessons.

I didn't use to do any exercise.

If your friend says *I didn't use to eat meat*, she also means ... *but I do now*.

1 Complete the sentences with *used to* and a suitable verb. Use words from the box to help.

> a cleaner   CDs   fast food   ~~football~~
> Geography   the cinema   thrillers   twenty

a Mike _used to play football_ , but he plays rugby now.

b This year Sheryl is studying Economics at university, but she _____ .

c Fiona reads lots of biographies now, but she _____ .

d Alec _____ , but these days he only eats healthy food.

e Lola _____ every Friday, but now she goes to comedy shows.

f Cristina _____ , but now she usually buys digital music.

g Karen is a hairdresser now, but she _____ .

h Yes! It's true! Roger has five Ferraris! You won't believe this, but he _____ .

2 Complete the questions with *did ... use to*.

a Jack works in the Town Hall now, but where _did he use to work?_

b Sheryl studies Politics at Cambridge University now, but what _____

c Mark is a teacher now, but what _____

d You live in New York now, but where _____

e She goes to the North Sports Centre now, but where _____

f Julia always comes to work by car these days, but how _____

g Ellen is dating Malik. Who _____

h Antonio reads a lot of science fiction. But what _____

3 Until last year, Luis lived in London, but then he moved to New York. Complete his sentences about London with *used to* or *didn't use to* and a verb from the box.

> drive   go   have   ~~like~~
> read   ride   take   work

a When I lived in London, I _didn't use to like_ the crowds and the noise. They drove me mad.

b I _____ in a city centre office block. I was on the 13th floor.

c Travelling took so much time! My journey to work _____ me nearly an hour.

d I _____ because the traffic was so bad. So I always left the car at home.

e Most days, I _____ by underground, but it was very crowded and unpleasant.

f I _____ a music player, so I got very bored on the journey.

g I _____ newspapers and books, but I found it hard to concentrate.

h After a while, I decided to buy a bike. I _____ it in the park on Sunday. But I was always too scared to cycle to work on it!

4 *ABOUT* YOU

Write some *used to* sentences about things you did in the past (but no longer do). You can use some verbs from the box if you need ideas.

> be   dream   eat   enjoy   go   have
> like   ~~make~~   play   think   visit

a When I was a very small child, _I used to make lots of 'shops'._

b At primary school, _____

c In the school playground, _____

d My family _____

e _____ , but I can't stand it now!

Explain that one thing happened before another

Past Perfect

Past Simple part

Past Perfect part

When they **arrived** at the theatre,

This is the beginning
of our story ...

the show **had started**.

... but this happened
before our story started.

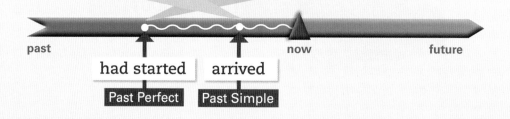

had started — Past Perfect

arrived — Past Simple

past · now · future

We use the Past Perfect to talk about an event that was completed before another event happened.

The Past Perfect is often used in sentences with the Past Simple.

I discovered that Laura and James had met before.

The Past Perfect is often used with *just* or *already*.

I'd just arrived at the seminar.

Piotr had already left for work when Magda woke up.

The Past Perfect often follows *after* or *when*, especially when we want to emphasise that one action finished before another started.

After we'd eaten, we all went for a walk in the park.

When the conference had finished, they closed the building.

Compare:

*When the police arrived, the robber **had** escaped.*

escaped — arrived

When the police arrived, the robber escaped.

arrived — escaped

The Past Simple part often starts with *before* or *by the time*.

Before I came to England, I'd never seen a red phone box.

By the time we arrived at the bus station, our coach had already left.

The sentence parts can be in a different order.

Our coach had already left by the time we arrived at the bus station.

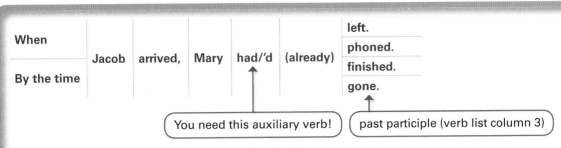

When		Jacob	arrived,	Mary	had/'d	(already)	left. phoned. finished. gone.
By the time							

You need this auxiliary verb!

past participle (verb list column 3)

You don't need to repeat 'd / had if the subject is the same, e.g.

She'd opened the door, (had) walked across the hall and (had) taken the necklace. (walked and taken
are both Past Perfect)

By the time she was 20, Martina had travelled the world and (had) lived in many foreign countries.

He had misread a road sign and (had) taken the wrong turning.

1 Write *1* next to the part of the sentence that happened **earlier** and *2* next to the part that happened **later**.

```
past            now         future
        1    2
```

a	_2_ Martin asked me	_1_	about the picture I had painted.
b	...... When I arrived,	......	Tim had already been to the shops.
c	...... I'd already printed six photos	......	when I noticed the problem.
d	...... He'd learnt Spanish	......	by the time he was 18.
e	...... When the guard returned,	......	the man had escaped.
f	...... Jemima had just come in	......	when the fire alarm rang.
g	...... My mother was really surprised	......	that we had made her a birthday cake.
h	...... Shelley had asked for a tea,	......	but they gave her a coffee.

2 Complete the sentences with the verbs in brackets in the Past Perfect.

a After I ___had seen___ (see) the film, I went home.

b By the time we got to the station, the train
_____ (leave).

c When the spaceship _____ (land), the army told the President.

d By the time we _____ (hear) the news, it was too late.

e When the postman came, everyone _____ (go) to work.

f Terry met Saskia after he _____ (sail) around the world.

g By the time she discovered the new facts, the book _____ (be) published.

h We started work on the report when we _____ (have) our lunch.

3 Complete the sentences. Use the words in brackets to give you ideas. Be careful! Sometimes you need the Past Simple, and sometimes the Past Perfect.

a When we got to the airport, *the check-in had already closed.* (the check-in / already / close)

b I'd just arrived home from work when _____ (my phone / ring)

c When we arrived at the stadium _____ (the football match / already / start)

d Tomoko had just pressed 'save' when _____ (her computer / crash)

e Giorgio _____ when he fell over! (just / score / a goal)

f The film had just finished on TV when _____ (Mia / come home)

I can ... **Talk about things I noticed, realised, saw, etc.**

Past Perfect with specific verbs

We often use the Past Perfect after verbs of saying and thinking.

realised | noticed | saw | heard | discovered | found | read

I **realised** that I **had left** my ID at home.

past

This happened further back in the past.

Terry noticed that the children had gone.
The guards saw that someone had walked across the yard.
We read that the fire had destroyed the whole building.

1 Join two sentences to make one. Start with the underlined part.

a She forgot her glasses. <u>Sheena suddenly realised</u>.
   Sheena suddenly realised that she had forgotten her glasses.

b Miranda left Sri Lanka. <u>I heard from my friends</u>.

c The new dresses all sold out in a few minutes. <u>We read on the website</u>.

d Someone changed the photo on the girl's identity card. <u>The examiner noticed</u>.

e Meg drove the whole way. <u>I realised</u>.

f Carla went. <u>I noticed</u>.

g Someone ate all the food. <u>I saw</u>.

h Chip chose the Physics course. <u>I heard</u>.

2 Look at the pictures and complete the sentences. (Different answers are possible.)

a
When Ian arrived in Istanbul, he realised that *he had lost his passport.*

b
When the Head of Marketing landed in South Africa, he discovered that the CEO

c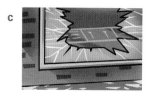
When they opened the shop in the morning they found that someone

d
While Cliff was waiting in the café he heard that Hastings United

More practice

because + Past Perfect

Why did you throw the tomatoes away?

Because they**'d gone** bad!

When we give a reason, we can use the Past Perfect to talk about a completed past event. We use the Past Perfect if there might be some confusion about which event happened first.

past — (1) reason ~~→ (2) event — now — future

(2) event	(1) reason
Why did Mum scream when she walked into the room?	*The children had poured shampoo all over the floor.*
Why was Paul so angry when he found his lost credit cards?	*Because he'd just phoned the bank to cancel them.*
Why did you look so worried when the teacher said 'Don't mix the chemicals together'?	*Because I'd mixed the chemicals together!*
Why did everyone walk out of the show?	*The projector had broken down.*

1 Write the reasons. Use the words in brackets in the correct form.

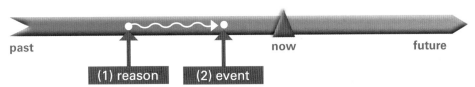

a Why didn't the girls go to the concert? (lose / their tickets)
Because they'd lost their tickets.

b Why did the boys miss three days of school? (catch / flu)

....

c Why didn't Julie get a certificate? (fail / exam)

....

d Why didn't Brett go into the cellar of the old house? (hear / lots of ghost stories!)

....

e Why did George buy a DVD of that film? (see / first twenty minutes)

....

f Why did Carol stop looking for a new flat? (find / one she really liked)

....

When I tell a story, I choose a 'start time' for the story.

The 'story start time'.

The other events happen after that story start time.

I arrived at the café. I bought a coffee. I sat down at a table. David called to cancel lunch.

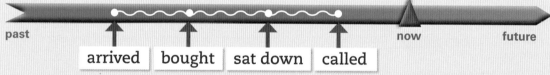

past   arrived   bought   sat down   called   now   future

We can change the 'story start time'. For example, I can tell the same story, but start when *David called to cancel lunch*. Everything that happened before my 'story start time' is in the Past Perfect.

David called to cancel lunch. Before that, I **had arrived** at the café, **bought** a coffee and **sat** down at a table.

This is the same story with the same events in the same order. The only difference is our idea about when the 'story' starts.

1 Read each sequence of events. Tell the story starting at the underlined part. Use the Past Perfect and *already*.

a I heard the news. <u>I met Jade in town</u>.
I met Jade in town. I had already heard the news.

b The secretary prepared everything. <u>The managers arrived</u>.

c We saw him at the office. <u>We said hello to Rufus at Julian's party</u>.

d Zak tried to call the office. <u>Jane called Zak's mobile</u>.

e The thieves took all the microchips and left. <u>We came in at 8 o'clock</u>.

f Sylvia went home. <u>The party went on till midnight</u>.

2 Rewrite the story so that the 'start' time is the underlined sentence.

Secret agent Scarlet Smith saw the enemy agent walk into the forest. She hid behind a tree and watched him. He took his phone out of his jacket and called a number. She heard his message and wrote it down. She watched him leave. <u>Scarlet Smith knew the secret</u>!

Secret agent Scarlet Smith knew the secret! She had seen the enemy agent walk into the forest.

3 **INTERNET QUIZ** 🔍

Here are some events from history. Write the verbs in brackets in the correct form and complete the sentences with the words in the box. Use the internet to help you.

> an Oscar   ~~CDs~~   ~~DVD~~   plays   the Great Eastern
> the Moon   the West Indies   Victoria

a Scientists invented the ...DVD... in 1995. People had ....*bought*.... (buy) the first ....CDs.... thirteen years before.

b When Shakespeare died in 1616, he had .... (write) 38 or more ....

c Harrison Schmitt and Eugene Cernan walked on .... in 1972. Before them, only ten other men had .... (go) there.

d Ferdinand Magellan's ship .... was the first to sail round the world. Columbus had already .... (discover) ....

e Martin Scorsese won .... for *The Departed* in 2007. He had .... (lose) five times before!

f When Isambard Kingdom Brunel designed .... , he had already .... (build) two huge ships.

Say that something happened before a certain time

Past Perfect with **by** and **before**

The meeting had finished **by 2 o'clock.**

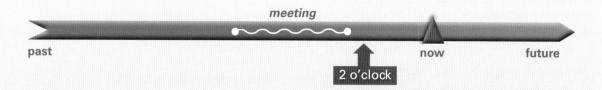

We don't know exactly when it finished. But we know it finished before a certain time.

By 9.00, she had painted the whole room.
*Our profits had improved **by the end of the year**.*

We can often make the grammar simpler by using the Past Simple instead of the Past Perfect without changing the meaning.
Sheila finished her work by midnight. = Sheila had finished her work by midnight.

1 Complete the sentences using the verbs in brackets in the correct form.

  a By the end of the day, we _'d delivered_ (deliver) all the letters.

  b The red team complained, but the referee _____ (blow) his whistle before they scored the goal.

  c The TV chefs _____ (cook) all the food before the end of the show.

  d The dragon _____ (go) to sleep by dawn.

  e By the time the lecturer started his third report, I _____ (have) enough!

  f By the time she started the lecture, half the students _____ (leave).

  g By 6 o'clock, every child _____ (wake up).

2 Complete the sentences using the Past Perfect. (Many different answers are possible.)

  a By the time I arrived at work, I realised that I _'d left my identity card at home._

  b By the end of last week, the children _____

  c Everyone _____ by 6.00 p.m. yesterday.

  d Before the party ended, my friends _____

  e By the time we reached the front of the queue, we _____

More practice

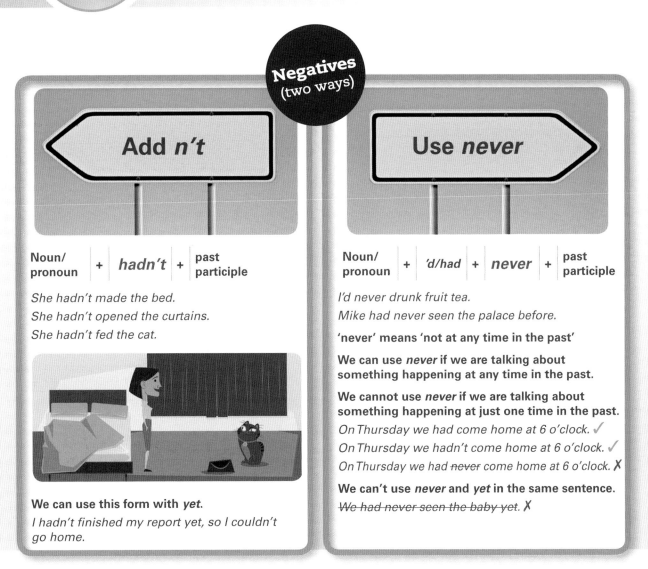

Negatives (two ways)

Add *n't*

| Noun/ pronoun | + | ***hadn't*** | + | past participle |

She hadn't made the bed.
She hadn't opened the curtains.
She hadn't fed the cat.

We can use this form with *yet*.

I hadn't finished my report yet, so I couldn't go home.

Use *never*

| Noun/ pronoun | + | *'d/had* | + | *never* | + | past participle |

I'd never drunk fruit tea.
Mike had never seen the palace before.

'never' means 'not at any time in the past'

We can use *never* if we are talking about something happening at any time in the past.

We cannot use *never* if we are talking about something happening at just one time in the past.

On Thursday we had come home at 6 o'clock. ✓
On Thursday we hadn't come home at 6 o'clock. ✓
On Thursday we had ~~never~~ come home at 6 o'clock. ✗

We can't use *never* and *yet* in the same sentence.

~~We had never seen the baby yet.~~ ✗

1 Reply to the questions using Past Perfect negative. Use the words in brackets.

a Why didn't you tell me what happened? (I / hear / news)
   I hadn't heard the news.

b Why didn't you say hello to Tina? (She / arrive)

c Why didn't Sean lend you his book? (He / find / it / yet)

d Why were they so frightened about the holiday? (They / fly / before)

e Why didn't you discuss the exercise? (They / do / it)

f Why didn't you give her the cake? (I / buy / it / yet)

2 Use the word pool to make five negative Past Perfect sentences. (Many different answers are possible.)

Challenge: Can you make a sentence with *exactly* ten words in it?

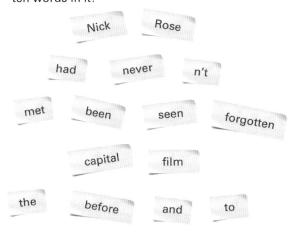

Nick   Rose   had   never   n't   met   been   seen   forgotten   capital   film   the   before   and   to

I can ... **Talk about the future**

will, **be going to**, Present Progressive

REVIEW UNIT
There's a lot more in *Visual Grammar A2*

Which grammar to talk about the future?

Was a **plan, arrangement** or **appointment** made *before now*?	**Present Progressive**	*I'm catching the 7.30 ferry from Caen.*
Was the future action decided **just now**?	**'ll / will**	*I'll answer this question!*
Was the future action decided **before** now?	**be going to**	*I'm going to see her later today.*
Can you **see, hear** or **understand something** now that tells you something is likely to happen in the future?	**be going to**	*It's going to crash!*
Do you **think** something will happen (i.e. you have a **prediction** about the future)?	**'ll / will**	*Robots will run the world.*
Do you have no idea which grammar to use?	**Try: be going to!**	*I'm going to get better.*

This won't always be right! But **be going to** is very commonly used!

Present Progressive

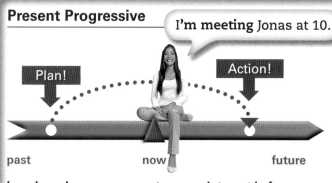

I'm meeting Jonas at 10.

Plan!   Action!

past   now   future

I made a plan, arrangement or appointment before now for something in the future.

For example, *I made a date with someone or booked a ticket*, etc.

We've booked tickets. We're going to see Les Miserables in June.

We often say when the arrangement will happen: 'at 10' 'on Tuesday' 'next week', etc.

I'm having my hair cut tomorrow.
I'm meeting Vala at 6.30.

---

be going to

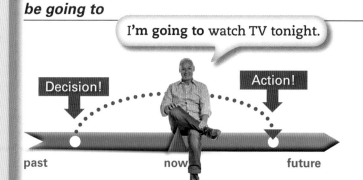

I'm going to watch TV tonight.

Decision!   Action!

past   now   future

I made a decision before now about an action in the future.

Also:
- Something you see (or hear) now tells you what will happen in the future:
  It's going to be dark soon.
  The car's going to break down.
- Predictions based on evidence:
  We're going to have a great party.
  It's all going to go wrong.

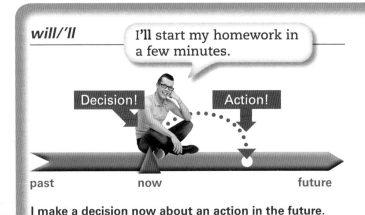

will/'ll

> I'll start my homework in a few minutes.

Decision! .... Action!

past — now — future

I make a decision now about an action in the future.

Also:
- **predictions of things you think will happen**

  I think that people will live on Mars in 20 years' time.

  I think that the weather will get worse!

  I'm sure you'll enjoy the film.

- **offers, promises, threats, requests**

  I'll get you a cup of tea.

  I'll pay you back tomorrow.

  I'll tell your father!

  Will you help me, please?

Negative = won't

Don't worry. You won't fail the exam.

BUT *I don't think the weather will get worse.*

~~I think the weather won't get worse.~~ ✗

Use *might* instead of *will* if you feel less certain it will happen:

We might win the match.

See Unit 51 for more information.

1 Write one word in each space. (Different answers are possible in some questions.)

a Look! That mouse is going __to__ eat your biscuit!

b We _____ having a marketing meeting after lunch today.

c Did you hear the weather forecast? Is it _____ to rain tonight?

d I think we _____ probably arrive at about midnight.

e Please _____ you speak to Thomas about the sales problem?

f Susan and Martin are _____ to Nepal on Sunday.

g There _____ be enough time to finish the work tonight. We'll finish it tomorrow.

h I might _____ the film again tonight! I really enjoyed it yesterday!

i I am certain that robots _____ control the whole world in 50 years' time.

2 Maria is a sales executive. What does she say in these situations? Complete her sentences with *be going to*, *'ll/will* or Present Progressive and the word in brackets. (Different answers to some questions are possible.)

a Maria is checking her diary. She wants to see her friend at 2 p.m. 'Oh no! I already have an appointment then! I __'m meeting__ (meet) a client at 2 o'clock.'

b Maria thinks the meeting might end before 3 p.m. She tells her friend, 'I think _____ (be) free by 3 o'clock!'

c At 1.55 p.m., the client arrives, but doesn't know where to go. The receptionist says, 'Don't worry. Follow me! I _____ (show) you! Maria's office is just down this corridor.'

d The client says, 'I checked with my boss. Our company _____ (order) 20,000 packets of Norona next week.'

e The client asks if he can have a second meeting next week. Maria says, 'I'm very sorry, but I _____ (work) in Geneva all next week.'

f Maria meets her friend in town. Maria looks at the dark clouds in the sky. She says, 'Oh dear, I think _____ (rain).'

g Her friend laughs and says, 'Don't worry! I'm sure _____ (stop) soon!'

3 Use the word pool to make six sentences about the future.

I | Matthew | you | it | her | 'm

're | 's | 'll | will | might | -ing

meet | rain | visit | play | go

stadium | football | the | to | in | on

at | next | month | Saturday | 3 o'clock

tomorrow

More practice

I can ...

Talk about timetabled events

Present Simple for timetabled events

GATE PASS ONLY
Ticket Type: ONE ADULT FIRST CLASS
Depart: 10:23 a.m.
From: LONDON TERMINALS
To: MUGFORD
Price: £17.50

Destination	Departure Time	Arrival Time
MUGFORD	10:23	11:48
calling at	:	
WEATHERLY	10:54	
EAST STOTTON	11:17	

12.15 Arrival at Mugford Hall
12.20 Speech
12.45 Departure to airport

FIRST CLASS
WINGS AIRLINE
Gate: 19 Gate Closes: 16:42 Seat: 27B
Gate: 19 Gate Closes: 16:42 Seat: 27B
Class: First Class
Departure time: 17:12
Departure: London LHR
Arrival: New York JFK
REF No: 00800597 524

I look forward to the conference tomorrow in New York. We'll meet at 9.00 – OK?
Best wishes,
Hans

So, Minister, let's run through today's schedule. Your train leaves at 10.23.

Does it stop at every station?

No. It's an express. It only stops at two stations.

When do I get to Mugford?

You arrive at 11.48. You get to the hall at 12.15. You make your speech at 12.20 and you finish by 12.45.

Then I go to Heathrow airport. Is that right?

Yes. Check in opens at 14.42. It closes two hours after that. Your plane takes off at 17.12. You land at 20.38.

And the next day I have a meeting?

Yes. It starts at 9.00 tomorrow morning and lasts all day. You fly home at 22.30.

How awful!

We use the Present Simple to talk about events in the future that:
• are in an official, published, fixed, regular timetable
  The plane takes off at 10.20.
or
• have been scheduled (e.g. they are in an advertisement, calendar, programme or itinerary with a time when they will happen)
  Our group arrives at the temple after lunch.
or
• for fixed events in your life and work
  I finish work at 2.00 on Fridays.

We don't usually use the Present Simple for personal arrangements that are not part of a fixed timetable or plan. The Present Progressive is better.
I ~~play football~~ with the boys tomorrow afternoon. ✗
I'm playing football with the boys tomorrow afternoon. ✓

Although you can use many verbs in the Present Simple with this meaning, some verbs are much more common:

| begin | end | start | last* | take* | be | open | close | finish | stop |

| come | go | return | take off | land | depart | leave | arrive | get** |

* *last* and *take*: Both verbs refer to the length of time from the beginning to the end of an event. We use *last* for a play, a song, etc. and *take* for a journey.
How long does the show last? It lasts two hours fifty minutes.
How long does the flight to New York take? It takes about six hours.

** *get*: If you ask 'When does it get to Bilbao?' you want to know 'When does it arrive in Bilbao?'.
When does the train get to London?

1 Choose the best verb for each gap and put it in the Present Simple. Use each verb twice.

> ~~arrive~~ close get last start

a The train __arrives__ at 17.20.
b Do we __arrive__ in Singapore before the weekend?
c I think all the shops _____ at 5.30.
d When does the film _____ ?
e Does the ferry _____ to France before teatime?
f How long does the conference _____ ?

g The competition _____ at midnight. If you enter after then, they won't look at your work!
h The lecture _____ at 9.30.
i Does the carnival _____ all week?
j I think this bus _____ to Nairobi early tomorrow morning.

2 Look at the ticket, timetable and theatre advertisement, then complete the sentences. (Different answers may be possible.)

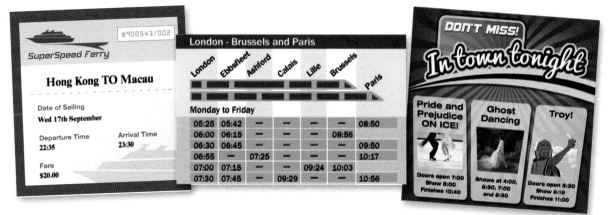

a The ferry __departs__ at 22.35.
b The ferry _____ to Macau at 23.30.
c Are you travelling on the first train on Friday? It _____ London at 5.25.
d The 5.25 train doesn't _____ at Ashford.
e How long does the journey to Paris _____ ?
f I'm going to catch the 7.30 train. It _____ at 10.56.

g Susie is taking me to the theatre. *Pride and Prejudice on Ice*! It _____ at 8.00.
h Oh, we're seeing *Ghost Dancing*. It _____ at 5.30, I think.
i I don't want to go to see *Troy*! Rebecca said it _____ more than four hours!

NOW
things that you think are possibly true now.
He might be right.

may is more common in formal written English.

← mean the same!

may and **might**

Use to talk about ... →

might is more common in everyday spoken English.

FUTURE
things that will possibly happen in the future.
They might be late.

When you use *may* or *might* you are not 100% certain.
I'll visit Jodi on my way home. → **100% definite**
I might go to the cinema tonight. → **99% or less**

1 ABOUT YOU

In each question, decide which sentence you agree with. Cross out the other ones.

a I will finish this exercise.
I might finish this exercise.
I won't finish this exercise.

b I will pass all my English exams.
I might pass all my English exams.
I won't pass all my English exams.

c In 2050, robots will control everything.
In 2050, robots might control everything.
In 2050, robots won't control everything.

d I will have lots of children.
I might have lots of children.
I won't have lots of children.

2 Answer each question using *may* and/or *might*. Use both ideas in brackets.

a 'The boys are very late! Where are they?' (Possibility 1: Their train is late. Possibility 2: They don't know the address.)
Their train might be late or they may not know the address.

b What will you do this afternoon? (Possibility 1: I'll watch a film. Possibility 2: I'll bake a cake.)

c Where's Vera? (Possibility 1: She's in the garden. Possibility 2: She isn't at home.)

d Do you know what James is going to make for supper? (Possibility 1: He'll make a pizza. Possibility 2: He won't cook anything!)

e Is Jerry feeling OK? He doesn't look very well. (Possibility 1: He has a cold. Possibility 2: He's stressed because of his work.)

f Edward doesn't have a suit. How can he go to the wedding? (Possibility 1: He can borrow a suit. Possibility 2: He can buy a cheap one from a second-hand shop.)

3 Look at the pictures and write five sentences using *may* or *might*. (Many different answers are possible.)

The policeman might talk to the teenager.
The woman might be a pickpocket.

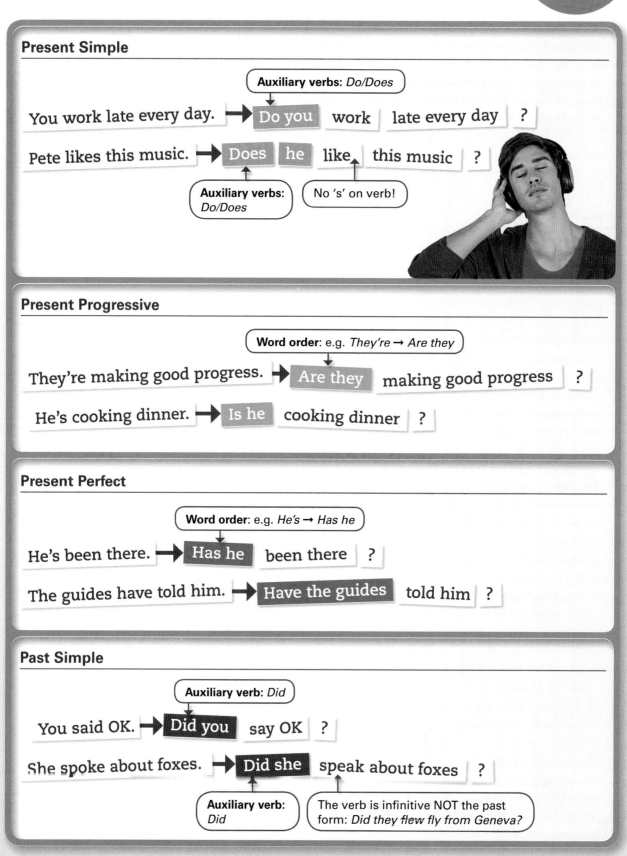

Present Simple

Auxiliary verbs: *Do/Does*

You work late every day. ➡ **Do you** work late every day ?

Pete likes this music. ➡ **Does** **he** like this music ?

Auxiliary verbs: *Do/Does*

No 's' on verb!

Present Progressive

Word order: e.g. *They're → Are they*

They're making good progress. ➡ **Are they** making good progress ?

He's cooking dinner. ➡ **Is he** cooking dinner ?

Present Perfect

Word order: e.g. *He's → Has he*

He's been there. ➡ **Has he** been there ?

The guides have told him. ➡ **Have the guides** told him ?

Past Simple

Auxiliary verb: *Did*

You said OK. ➡ **Did you** say OK ?

She spoke about foxes. ➡ **Did she** speak about foxes ?

Auxiliary verb: *Did*

The verb is infinitive NOT the past form: *Did they flew fly from Geneva?*

Past Progressive

Word order: e.g. *Heidi was* → *Was Heidi*

Heidi was joking! → **Was Heidi** joking ?

The kids were making snowmen. → **Were the kids** making snowmen ?

be going to

Word order: e.g. *She's* → *Is she*

She's going to be late. → **Is she** going to be late ?

They're going to make a film. → **Are they** going to make a film ?

---

1 Make *yes/no* questions to ask Jane. Use the words in brackets. Then name the tense.

Jane's statements		Your questions	Name the tense
Dave works in a garage.	(every day)	a *Does he work there every day?*	*Present Simple*
Sarah's making supper.	(spaghetti)	b *Is she making spaghetti?*	*Present Progressive*
The children play lots of computer games.	(after school)	c	
The athletes are going to practise.	(in the gym)	d	
The visitors were waiting.	(for me)	e	
Patricia has flown to the USA.	(Washington)	f	
Ian caught a train at Victoria station.	(a train to Brighton)	g	
Vicky likes Italian food.	(pasta)	h	

2 These questions are all in the Present Progressive. Change them to the tense in brackets.

a Is your girlfriend meeting us at the shops? (*be going to*)
Is your girlfriend going to meet us at the shops?

b Are the boys ringing their parents? (Present Perfect)
Have the boys rung their parents?

c Is John having a shower? (Past Progressive)

d Is your mum booking her plane tickets online? (Past Simple)

e Are the engineers working every day? (Present Simple)

f Are they visiting Australia? (Present Perfect)

g Are you feeling cold? (Past Simple)

h Is that plane taking off? (*be going to*)

i Are the chickens waking up? (Present Perfect)

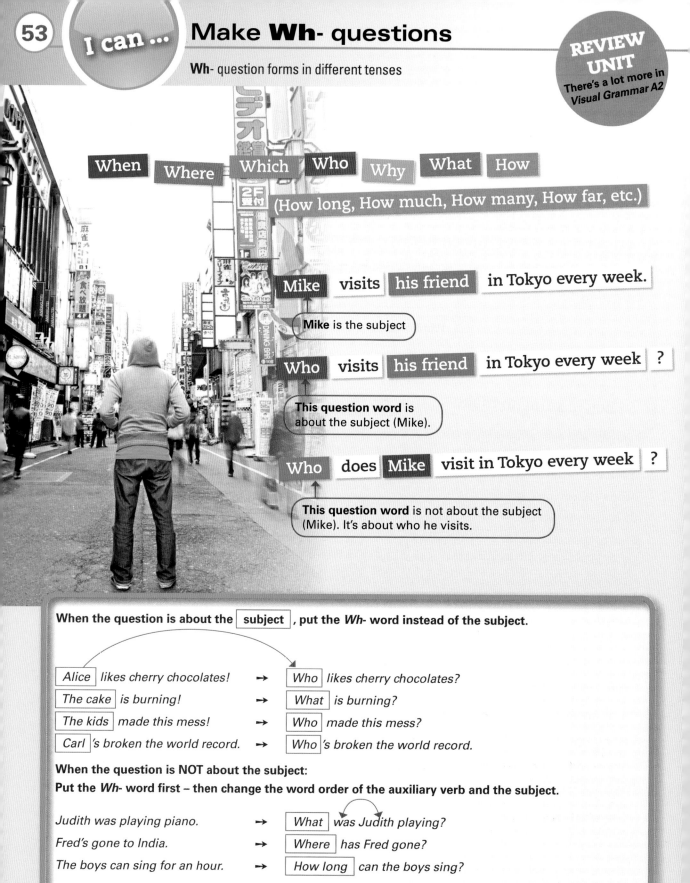

When | Where | Which | Who | Why | What | How

(How long, How much, How many, How far, etc.)

Mike | visits | his friend | in Tokyo every week.

(**Mike** is the subject)

Who | visits | his friend | in Tokyo every week | ?

(**This question word** is about the subject (Mike).)

Who | does | Mike | visit in Tokyo every week | ?

(**This question word** is not about the subject (Mike). It's about who he visits.)

When the question is about the | subject | , put the *Wh-* word instead of the subject.

| Alice | likes cherry chocolates! → | Who | likes cherry chocolates?

| The cake | is burning! → | What | is burning?

| The kids | made this mess! → | Who | made this mess?

| Carl | 's broken the world record. → | Who | 's broken the world record.

When the question is NOT about the subject:

Put the *Wh-* word first – then change the word order of the auxiliary verb and the subject.

Judith was playing piano. → | What | was Judith playing?

Fred's gone to India. → | Where | has Fred gone?

The boys can sing for an hour. → | How long | can the boys sing?

If there is no auxiliary verb, use *do/does/did*.

She grows potatoes → | What | does she grow?

They played cards. → | Why | did they play cards?

1 These questions are all in the Present Progressive. Change them to the tense in brackets.

a Where are you going? (Past Simple)
Where did you go?

b What is he doing? (Present Perfect)
What has he done?

c Why is Jake crying? (Past Progressive)

d Who is cooking lunch? (*be going to*)

e Who is flying to Las Vegas? (Past Simple)

f What are they stealing? (Present Perfect)

g When is she writing her blog post? (Past Simple)

h What is Greg eating for lunch? (Present Simple)

i Who is Tom speaking to? (Present Perfect)

j Who is speaking to Tom? (Present Perfect)

k Who is Tom speaking to? (Past Simple)

l Who is speaking to Tom? (Past Simple)

2 Sir Roderick Fimble, the famous explorer, has just come back from an exciting expedition. Marilyn asks him questions on her chat show. Complete her questions with the words in brackets.

So, Sir Roderick, tell me ...

Marilyn		Sir Roderick
a How long (you / be) back in England?	*How long have you been back in England?*	About two weeks.
b Where (you / go) last year?	*Where did you go last year?*	I sailed to a mysterious island in the South Pacific.
c Why (you / go) there?		Because there were lots of strange stories about it.
d What (you / discover)?		We found a monster!
e Really? What (it / look like)?		It was like a giant gorilla. Like King Kong.
f What (it / do) when you found it?		It was sitting in a field eating fruit!
g What (you / do) with it?		We caught it. We brought it with us back to England!
h No! I don't believe it! Where (it / live) now?		It lives in our laboratory! And right now, it ... I mean SHE ... is waiting at the back of the studio!
i Agh! How long (she / be) there?		Since this morning! Don't worry! She's not dangerous.
j Are you sure? What (make) that noise?		That's probably Shirley. Ah yes ... she's coming now.
k Help! What (she / do) to us?		Don't panic. She won't hurt you!
l How (you / know)?		She's a very gentle, friendly monster! She won't hurt you! Shirley! Come and say 'Hello' to Marilyn ...

Ask questions when I think I know the answer

Question tags

48

You're Paloma Revez, **aren't you?**

You were in *Changing News*, **weren't you?**

She makes GREAT films, **doesn't she?**

Mike Madman is her boyfriend, **isn't he?**

You left him, **didn't you?**

You'll go back, **won't you?**

46

Your fans are crazy, **aren't they?**

It's time to leave, **isn't it?**

If the sentence has *be* as the main verb:

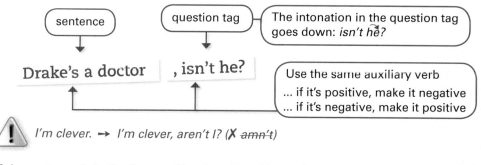

sentence → question tag

The intonation in the question tag goes down: *isn't he?*

Drake's a doctor , isn't he?

Use the same auxiliary verb
... if it's positive, make it negative
... if it's negative, make it positive

⚠ *I'm clever.* → *I'm clever, aren't I?* (✗ *amn't*)

If the sentence is in the Present Simple or Past Simple (i.e. there is no auxiliary verb):

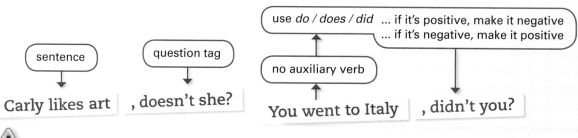

use *do / does / did* ... if it's positive, make it negative
... if it's negative, make it positive

sentence → question tag

no auxiliary verb

Carly likes art , doesn't she?   You went to Italy , didn't you?

⚠ *She has new glasses.* → *She has new glasses, doesn't she?* (✗ *hasn't*)
She's got new glasses. → *She's got new glasses, hasn't she?*

If the sentence has an auxiliary verb:

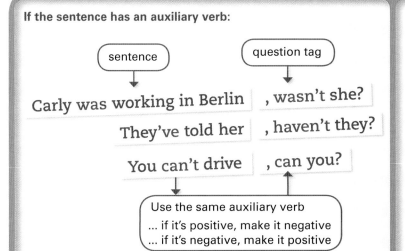

sentence — question tag

Carly was working in Berlin **, wasn't she?**

They've told her **, haven't they?**

You can't drive **, can you?**

Use the same auxiliary verb
... if it's positive, make it negative
... if it's negative, make it positive

Use question tags when you think that you already know the right answer!

We aren't late, are we?

You work for Gulliver Chemicals, don't you?

You don't eat fish, do you?

This train goes to Penzance, doesn't it?

We also use question tags for social chat.

It's lovely weather, isn't it?

Oh, she's wearing a lovely dress, isn't she?

He cooks very well, doesn't he?

 He used to work here. → *He used to work here, didn't he? (✗ usedn't)*

Some students use *isn't it* all the time. This is incorrect.

These are my books, isn't it? → *These are my books, aren't they?*

You love lemonade, isn't it? → *You love lemonade, don't you?*

Mary's your best friend, isn't it? → *Mary's your best friend, isn't she?*

---

1 Make the sentences into questions by adding question tags.

a This is a beautiful beach.
This is a beautiful beach, isn't it?

b The boys were late.

c You didn't buy a new hat.

d These books are exciting.

e He's got a discount ticket.

f We went there last summer.

g You're not the new accountant.

h I'm player number one.

2 Choose the right question for each space in the conversations.

> He's going to make the cakes, isn't he?
> The car was parked outside, wasn't it?
> The clean towels are in the drawer, aren't they?
> The lessons weren't cancelled, were they?
> They left the show early, didn't they?
> This is the right way, isn't it?
> ~~You're Lindsay Watson, aren't you?~~

a *You're Lindsay Watson, aren't you?* Yes, I am.

b .... Yes, it is.

c .... No, they aren't.

d .... Yes, it was.

e .... Yes, he is.

f .... Yes, they did.

g .... No, they weren't.

3 Some students have made mistakes with question tags! Correct the sentences if they are wrong.

a They went into town, ~~isn't it?~~
They went into town, didn't they?

b You bought some bread, isn't it?

c The printers were all damaged, isn't it?

d The printers are all damaged, isn't it?

e The printer isn't damaged, isn't it?

f The printer is damaged, isn't it?

What's your name?

Um. Hello. Have we met?

Excuse me. Could you tell me your name?

Yes, of course. I'm Petra.

How old are you?

Well ...

Would you mind telling me how old you are?

I'm nearly 30.

Direct questions

Indirect questions

How much do you earn?

Er ... sorry, do I know you?

I was wondering how much you earn.

Ha, ha, ha. I'd rather not say!

What do you do?

Um ...

May I ask you what you do?

I'm a marketing executive.

Who's that?

I wonder if you know who that is.

I think that's Margo – the council leader.

When does this event finish?

Have you got any idea when this event finishes?

I think it's about 10 o'clock.

Wh- questions

Where is the Post Office? ← (direct question)

This is not incorrect English, but ... if you are speaking to a stranger in a formal situation, it might sound a little rude. Indirect questions sound more polite.

(Excuse me.)

Use **Excuse me** if you are interrupting or starting a conversation with a stranger.

Can you tell me	
Could you tell me	
Can/May I ask you	
Do you know	where the Post Office is? ← ⚠ NOT question word order!
Have you got any idea	
Would you mind telling me	
I wonder if you know	
I was wondering	where the Post Office is.
I don't know	

Yes/no questions

Does Mr Finch live here? ← direct questions
Are they waiting for someone?

Can you tell me	⚠️ Use *if* or **whether**
Could you tell me	
Can/May I ask you	**Mr Finch lives here?**
Do you know	
Have you got any idea	**they are waiting for someone?**
Would you mind telling me	*if / whether*
I wonder if you know	**Mr Finch lives here.**
I was wondering	
I don't know	**they are waiting for someone.**

Do/Does questions

Where does the bus go from? ← direct question

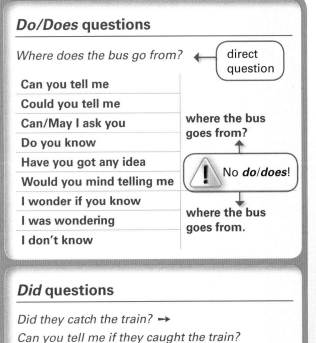

Can you tell me
Could you tell me
Can/May I ask you
Do you know
Have you got any idea
Would you mind telling me
I wonder if you know
I was wondering
I don't know

where the bus goes from?

⚠️ No *do/does!*

where the bus goes from.

Did questions

Did they catch the train? →
Can you tell me if they caught the train?

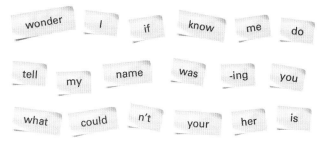

⚠️ No *did!*   ⚠️ Put the verb in the past!

1 Change the direct questions into indirect questions. Start with the word(s) given.

a How many children have you got?
I was wondering how many children you've got.

b Where's the train station?
Do you ....

c When does this shop close?
Excuse me. Could you ....

d Did you enjoy your holiday?
I was ....

e What mark did Alice get?
Would you ....

f Did the meeting finish successfully?
Can you ....

g Does the CEO want everyone at the meeting?
I wonder ....

h What subject did you study at university?
May I ....

2 What would you say in these situations? (Different answers are possible.)

a You're lost in town. You want to find the Electric cinema. Ask a stranger.
Excuse me. Do you know where the Electric cinema is?

b You're in a restaurant. You really want to know the football score! Ask your waiter.
....

c Your teacher looks very busy, marking work. You want to ask her if you passed the test.
....

d You're waiting for a bus at a small countryside bus stop. Ask a stranger if he knows when the next bus is due.
....

e You meet a pregnant colleague at the water cooler. Ask her whether she knows if it's a boy or a girl.
....

f You're in a café. A man has one of the café's newspapers on the table, but he isn't reading it. Ask him if you could look at it.
....

3 Use the word pool to make five or more indirect questions. (You can use words more than once!)

wonder I if know me do

tell my name was -ing you

what could n't your her is

= the exact words someone says		= you tell someone what was said	The pronouns change too!

Direct speech		Reported speech
Use quotation marks ' '		No quotation marks
		The verbs change to the past ... because you are reporting words spoken in the past (even if it was just a few minutes ago).
Present Simple	→	Past Simple
Present Progressive	→	Past Progressive
am / is	→	was
are	→	were
do / does	→	did
can	→	could

The pronouns change too!
I → she/he, we → they
my → his/her, etc.

'I have a new car.' →
He said he had a new car.

past

'I'm enjoying my holiday.' →
She said that she was enjoying her holiday.

'We can come with you!' →
They said that they could come with us.

You can use that or miss it out. It's the same.

Mike said he was working. =
Mike said that he was working.

1 Helen said these things to you on the phone just now. Report the sentences to your friend, Mark.

a 'I'm working in the garden.'
She said that she was working in the garden.

b 'I'm getting ready for the children's party.'
....

c 'I want to make some decorations.'
....

d 'I don't feel tired.'
....

e 'The garden looks beautiful.'
....

f 'I'm not organising any games.'
....

g 'I hope that Mark likes the hot weather.'
....

2 The sentences are from a newspaper report about a politician. What were his exact original words?

a He said that he regretted his actions.
'I regret my actions.'

b He said that he agreed with the Prime Minister's decision.
....

c He said that he enjoyed his work.
....

d He said that he was waiting for more information.
....

e He said that he didn't believe in Father Christmas.
....

f He said that he was resigning next week.
....

More practice

I can ...   Report people's ideas about the future

Reported speech: **would**, **might** and **was going to**

They'll win the game.

He said they **would** win the game.

We may arrive late.

They said that they **might** arrive late.

Direct speech		Reported speech
will/would	→	would
am/is/are going to	→	was/were going to
may/might	→	might

We're going to have a barbecue!

I'm going to watch TV.

She said that she **was going to** watch TV.

They said that they **were going to** have a barbecue.

1 Complete the reports about what John said.

a 'I'll buy some cheese!'
John said that *he would buy some cheese.*

b 'The team is going to be late.'
John said that ....

c 'I may go to London.'
John said that ....

d 'The plane will arrive soon.'
John said that ....

e 'The children are going to listen to some music.'
John said that ....

f 'The computer may not work.'
John said that ....

2 In the film *Alien Escape*, two heroes have been captured by evil aliens! Read the description of their conversation. Then complete the film script.

> Miranda said that she was going to escape through the air pipes – but Harry looked worried. He said the alien guard might see her. Miranda said that she was going to be very quiet. Harry sighed and said that her plan would go wrong. He would think of a better idea.
> After a few minutes, he said he'd got a new plan – he was going to pretend to be ill. The guard would hear him and come in to their prison cell. Miranda agreed with the plan and said that when the guard came in, she would run out quickly and lock the door. Harry complained that he would be trapped in the cell with the guard! Miranda told him not to worry. She would come back to rescue him later.

Miranda: I *'m going to escape through* ª the air pipes.

Harry: The alien guard *may see* ᵇ you!

Miranda: I .... ᶜ quiet.

Harry: Your .... ᵈ wrong.
I .... ᵉ idea ... I .... ᶠ plan.
I .... ᵍ ill. The guard .... ʰ cell.

Miranda: OK. When the guard comes in, I .... ⁱ door.

Harry: But I .... ʲ guard.

Miranda: Don't worry! I .... ᵏ later.

3 INTERNET QUIZ

First, decide what the original words were. Then use the internet to find out who said these words.

a He said that everything was going to (= 'gonna') be alright.
'Everything's gonna be alright!' Bob Marley
(Jamaican singer)

b He said that we would remember not the words of our enemies, but the silence of our friends.

....

c He said he would let you be in his dreams, if he could be in yours.

....

More practice

109

Report people's stories about past events

Reported speech (past tenses)

Hi Annette,

I've been to a Lana Del Rey concert!

I queued for hours to get a place right at the front.

It was a great show.

Yes. I'd seen her before.

Did you speak to Sally?

She said that she'd been to a Lana Del Rey concert!

She said she had queued for hours to get a place right at the front.

She said it had been a great show.

She said that she had seen her before.

or

She said that she's been to a Lana Del Rey concert!

She said she queued for hours to get a place right at the front.

She said it was a great show.

She said that she had seen her before.

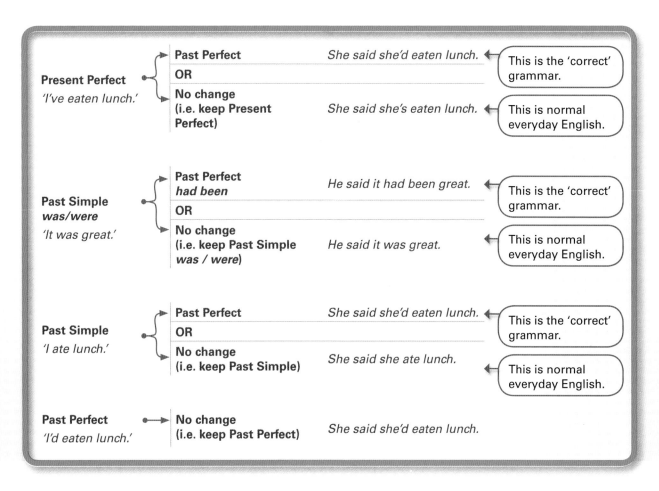

1 Marco said these things to you on the phone. Report them to your friend Simon. (Different answers are possible.)

a I've seen Danny.
He said he'd seen Danny.

b I've watched a great DVD.

c I'd never seen a 3D film before.

d It was great!

e I forgot to check the news about the Oscars.

f I went to the film premiere.

g I said hello to Jason Isaacs.

2 Read these sentences from an interview with a teacher. Then write a report of each sentence. Be careful! Most verbs are in the past – but some are in the present!

a My class has worked very hard on their winter project.
He said that his class had worked very hard on their winter project.

b They have chosen really interesting topics.

c The students had never done anything like it before.

d I think that the results are high quality.

e Some students displayed their projects in the school hall.

f I like the one about volcanoes most.

Reported speech with **said**, **told**

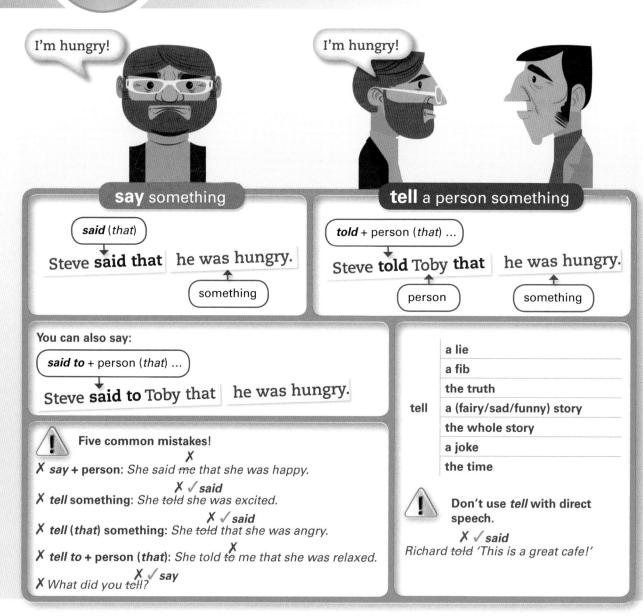

1 Complete the sentences with *said* or *told*.

a Greg ___told___ the staff about the new rules.

b The children .... their teacher that the rabbit was lost.

c She .... that she was watching TV.

d Mr Griffiths .... us there was a real alien at the museum!

e Yesterday I .... that answer b was correct, but I was wrong!

f Yesterday I .... you that answer b was correct, but I was wrong!

g Yesterday I .... to class 2D that that answer b was correct, but I was wrong.

2 Complete the sentences with *say*, *said*, *tell* or *told*.

a He didn't ___tell___ us Mary was getting married!

b The giant .... the elf to visit him.

c He .... he was interested in the new project.

d We .... you! You didn't listen!

e When they asked you about the money, what did you .... them?

f When they asked you about the money, what did you ....?

g When they asked you about the money, what did you .... to them?

h The mountaineer .... us the whole story after he was rescued.

i Michael knocked at the door. Giselle opened it and .... 'Oh, Michael! I'm so glad you've come.'

More practice

Are you in the same class?

He asked me **if** we were in the same class.

Who's your teacher?

He asked me **who** my teacher was.

---

yes/no question → use *whether or if*

'Can I go to the gym?' → I asked whether I could go to the gym.

'Do you want ice cream?' → Sharon asked if we wanted ice cream.

wh- question → use *why / who / what / when*, etc.

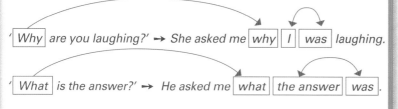

'Why are you laughing?' → She asked me why I was laughing.

'What is the answer?' → He asked me what the answer was.

⚠ Don't use *say* or *tell* for reported questions. Use *ask*.

'Where do you live?' →
She <u>asked</u> where he lived.

No question mark!

Use *say*, *reply* or *answer* to answer.

'I live in Lima.' →
He <u>said/replied/ answered</u> that he lived in Lima.

---

1 Write the original questions.

a She asked me where I was going.
'Where are you going?'

b He asked why the bridge was shut.

c Marie asked who the man was.

d Mike asked whether we liked chips.

e The teachers asked where our group was working.

f I asked if you were planning to make dinner.

g Terry asked whether his painting was good.

h The policeman asked me if I could help him.

2 Report the questions. (Different answers are possible.)

a Sandy asked me, 'Where is your hat?'
Sandy asked me where my hat was.

b Debbie asked me, 'What's the time?'

c Judy asked me, 'Where did the cats go?'

d Sam asked me, 'Do you like garlic?'

e Ted asked me, 'Who's your doctor?'

f Marc asked me, 'When did the children leave?'

g Susie asked me, 'Do you want some apple pie?'

h Mick asked me, 'Can you play the guitar?'

We can meet at the farm.

I **thought** we could meet at the farm.

I CAN do this exam.

I **knew** that I could do that exam.

We can report thoughts as well as speech.

Reported thoughts

thought

knew

believed

decided

Which drink do I want? I want ... lemonade!

I **decided** that I wanted lemonade.

They're real.

When I was small, I **believed** that fairies were real.

1 Complete the reports about what Emma thought.

a 'I'll get a pizza!'
Emma thought that she would get a pizza.

b 'It's a great party'
Emma thought that ....

c 'The children are happy.'
Emma believed that ....

d 'It's the wrong answer.'
Emma knew that ....

e 'My team is going to win.'
Emma believed that ....

f 'It's too cold to go out.'
Emma decided that ....

g 'I'll buy a new chair.'
Emma decided that ....

2 *ABOUT* YOU

Write some true sentences about yourself.

a When I was ___*a very young child*___ I believed
that ___*grown-ups were very clever.*___

b When I was .... I believed
that ....

c When I was .... I thought
that ....

d When I was .... I knew that
....

e When I was .... I decided
that ....

f When I was .... my mother
thought that ....

g When I was in .... class my
teacher thought that ....

More practice

Reported speech with **complained, explained, announced, whispered**

Jane **complained** that her food was boring.

complain = say that you think something is wrong or unsatisfactory

She **explained** that she needed more ice cream and cake.

explain = give information in a clear way that helps people understand

She **announced** that she was leaving home.

announce = give information clearly, loudly and formally (usually to a group of people)

Mum **whispered** that it was time for bed.

whisper = say very quietly in someone's ear

When we report we usually use *say* or *tell* – but we can make our reporting more interesting by choosing a really good reporting verb.

Some more verbs:

add = say something more about the same subject
repeat = say something again
reply = say something in response to something someone has said
warn = say that there is something dangerous or a problem
promise = tell a person that you will definitely do something

1 Report the sentences, starting with the words given. Use *complained, whispered, announced* or *explained*.

a

This soup is terrible.

John *complained that the soup was terrible.*

b

I will resign tomorrow.

The minister ....

c

You can't eat sweets all day ... they are bad for you.

Tim's father ....

d

I love you!

He ....

e

The shopping centre is closing at 8 o'clock.

They ....

f

The word 'location' means 'place'.

The lecturer ....

g

This flat is very dirty.

Jacqui ....

h

I need to go to the toilet.

Sam ....

2 <u>Underline</u> the correct verb.

a The student leader *asked* <u>announced</u> / *complained* that they would start a protest meeting at 2 o'clock.

b David walked over to the customer service desk and *complained* / *replied* / *told* that the chocolate machine wasn't working.

c When Susie asked for a pen, Tom *complained* / *told* / *replied* that there was one on the table.

d My three-year-old daughter went up to the policeman and *replied* / *asked* / *whispered* that she wanted a cookie.

If we add too many mushrooms, the cost rises.

It's simple! If people don't like the taste, they don't buy our pizza.

If I tell my husband about my work, he just yawns and turns on the TV!

Ha ha!

If you fly across the USA, you pass through a number of time zones.

Mike – listen! If you go by train, it takes longer – but you arrive fresher!

Yes. Sorry. Yes. If you phone the office before 9 a.m., you get the answerphone. That's right.

(If this is true ...) (then this will always happen)

| **If** | **something happens** | **(then)** | **something else happens** |

⬆ Present Simple   ⬆ Present Simple

If costs rise, then prices rise.
If you read a lot of books, your vocabulary increases.
If you heat the compound to 85°, it turns green.

or

| **something happens** | **if** | **something else happens** |

⬆ Present Simple   ⬆ Present Simple

Prices rise if costs rise.
Your vocabulary increases if you read a lot of books.
The compound turns green if you heat it to 85°.
We don't use a comma.

Negatives are possible:
If the mixture isn't exactly right, it burns.
If visitors don't sign the form, we don't let them in.

Use this conditional for things that are always or generally true (i.e. past, present and future), e.g.

Explaining how machines, organisations, etc. work	*If you push this button, a cup comes out.*
	If anyone asks for more information, we look it up on Wikipedia.
	The correction shows in a pop-up box if you make a spelling mistake.
Saying what happens if there is a problem	*If you don't pay today, the fine goes up to £100.*
	The machine stops if there isn't enough oil.
Business, religious or philosophical truths and guidelines	*If you treat the customer well, the customer comes back.*
	If you get more things, you want more things.
Scientific or economic facts, rules and laws	*If you add this acid, it explodes!*
	The government falls if inflation rises too high.

1 Bruce, the Managing Director of Comfy Chairs, is talking about his business beliefs. Match the beginnings and ends of his sentences.

a If you set your prices too high,　　1 then he's right.
b If you ask a good question,　　2 I rewrite them.
c If you are honest to your employees,　　3 no one buys your products.
d If the rules don't work,　　4 you get good answers.
e If the customer thinks he's right,　　5 they respect you more.

2 Petra is a scientist at the Leafline Research Foundation. Match the beginnings and ends of her sentences.

a If a researcher discovers anything important,　　1 all our research stops.
b If you drop any liquids on the floor,　　2 they tell everyone at the morning meeting.
c If the money runs out,　　3 we all leave the building immediately.
d If the government gives us extra cash,　　4 the cleaners clean it up immediately.
e If the alarm sounds,　　5 we employ more researchers.

3 Craig is a life coach. He is giving advice about getting fit. Match the beginnings and ends of his sentences.

a If you exercise regularly,　　1 it adds to the calories.
b If people stop using the lifts,　　2 it improves their general health.
c If you put milk in your coffee,　　3 you get fitter.
d If overweight people lose a kilo or two,　　4 you feel tired all day.
e If you sleep too much,　　5 the stairs give them lots of extra exercise.

4 *INTERNET* QUIZ

Complete the sentences. Use nouns and verbs from the box. Use a dictionary or the internet to help you.

Nouns
car DVD eyes recording ~~salt~~ snow water

Verbs
boil ~~dissolve~~ melt rewind see start stop

a If you mix salt and water, the *salt dissolves.*
b .... if you heat it to 100°.
c If you press '<<', the ....
d If you press '•', the ....

e If the weather becomes warmer, the ....
f The .... if you put your foot on the brake.
g If you don't eat enough vitamin A, your .... can't .... in the dark.

More practice

Tell people what to do if something happens

Conditional type 0 with imperative

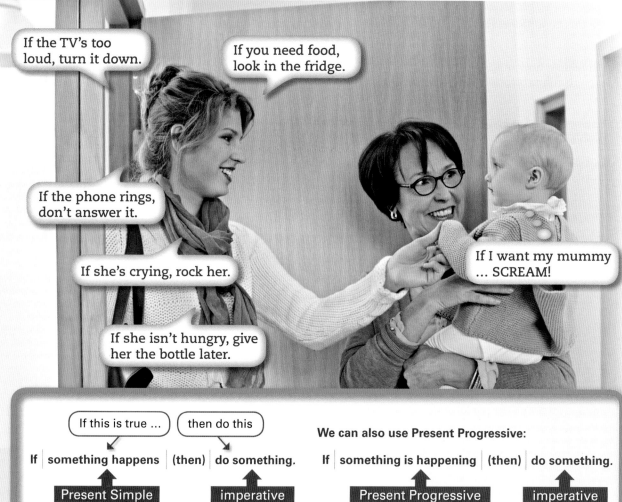

If the TV's too loud, turn it down.

If you need food, look in the fridge.

If the phone rings, don't answer it.

If I want my mummy ... SCREAM!

If she's crying, rock her.

If she isn't hungry, give her the bottle later.

If this is true ... → then do this

| If | something happens | (then) | do something. |

↑ Present Simple   ↑ imperative

If you feel cold, turn the heater on.
If the microwave doesn't work, hit it.

We can also use Present Progressive:

| If | something is happening | (then) | do something. |

↑ Present Progressive   ↑ imperative

If the baby is screaming, phone me!
If you're not enjoying the TV, try one of the DVDs.

---

1 Complete each sentence with an imperative from the box.

> call your doctor immediately
> put a cartoon film on for them
> put on your warm hat and scarf
> refill the tank
> try again ~~turn it off~~

a If Peter says that the music is too loud, *turn it off.*
b If the petrol runs out, ...
c If it starts to snow while you are out,
....
d If you become ill over the next 48 hours,
....
e If the children get bored, ...
f If at first you don't succeed, ...

2 Complete the sentences. (Different answers are possible.)

a If you want to have some exercise,
come for a walk with me.
....
b If you hear the fire alarm,
....
c If your hotel room isn't clean,
....
d If the fat in the frying pan starts burning,
....
e If the children are playing in the garden,
....
f If Michael asks you for the Insurance Folder,
....

More practice

when, before, after, while, until

Future events

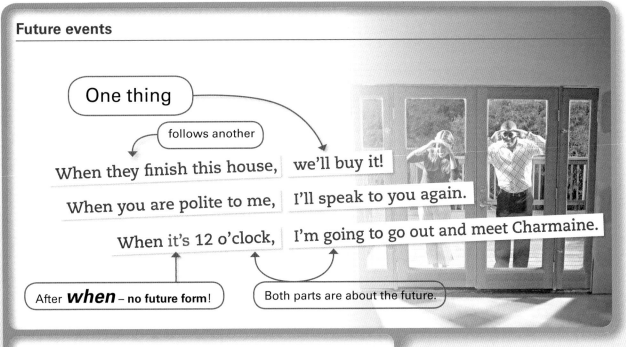

One thing

follows another

When they finish this house, | we'll buy it!

When you are polite to me, | I'll speak to you again.

When it's 12 o'clock, | I'm going to go out and meet Charmaine.

After **when** – no future form!

Both parts are about the future.

✗ **when** + will   ✓ **when** + present

When I will get to Paris, I'll call you.
When the weather will improves, we can visit the National Park.
I'll tell you what I think when I will see your report.

Also: *before, after, while, until*

Before I will go home, I'm going to pop in to Grandma's.
After Judy will prints the form, she'll take it to the Post Office.
I'm going to check on Google while you will make a cup of tea.
We'll stay on this road until we will reach Frankfurt.

---

1 Cross out *'ll / will* in each sentence **if** it is wrong.

a When you'll come home, I'll cook supper.
b I'll read the book before I will watch the film.
c After you will phone Terry, we can go out.
d Marty will tell you about the meeting when you will come into the office.
e Susie will wait until I will finish this job.
f I'll buy you a present when you will tell me what you want!

2 Complete the sentences. Use the verbs in brackets.

a While you ___are___ (be) in Australia, you __'ll see__ (see) Uluru.
b When the rocket _____ (take off), there _____ (be) an incredibly loud noise.
c When supper _____ (be) ready, Sheila _____ (call) everyone.
d We _____ (wait) here until the game _____ (finish).
e The company _____ (pay) your expenses after you _____ (send) your receipts.
f I _____ (be) really angry when they _____ (close) our nursery.
g The host _____ (introduce) everyone when the show _____ (start).
h Everyone _____ (be) very happy when Quinn _____ (arrive).
i We _____ (catch) the bus before it _____ (start) to rain.

Conditional type 1

This will happen

but only if this happens!

If I get that new job, I'll move to Madrid.

If they don't arrive late, we're going to start the meeting at 10 a.m.

If they agree, Sue and Billy can swap desks.

After **if** – no future form!

Both parts are about the future.

✗ **if** + ~~will~~
✓ **if** + present

If I ~~will~~ fail the test, I'll take it again.

I'll call you if I ~~will~~ find your glasses.

If he drops them ...

When he gets out ...

If = I think this may possibly happen (but it may not)

When = I think this will definitely happen

1 Underline *when* or *if*.

a My manager will be here this afternoon. I'll discuss it *when* / *if* he arrives.

b The washing machine takes about 50 minutes. *When* / *If* it finishes, the clothes will still be wet.

c Sally said she may have a spare suitcase at home. She said she'll check. She'll phone me *when* / *if* she finds one.

d Let's meet at midday. I'll call you *if* / *when* I'm late.

e Let's meet in the park. *When* / *If* it rains, we can meet in the coffee house.

2 Cross out *'ll* / *will* if it is wrong.

a I'll tell Joss if I ~~will~~ meet her.

b If we will arrive before midday, we'll have lunch with Greig.

c Mac will check the database if you'll ask him.

d If all the children will come into the classroom, Mrs Morris will explain the plan.

e If we will hurry, we'll be at the theatre in time.

f I'll tidy the chairs if you will move the tables.

3 Complete the sentences. Use the verbs in brackets.

a If you __visit__ (visit) Norris tomorrow, he __'ll give__ (give) you all the files you need.

b If Margaret .... (come) to the restaurant, we .... (make) a decision then.

c Those boxes .... (fall down) if you .... (put) more on top.

d If it .... (snow) this morning, we .... (cancel) the meeting.

e If your temperature .... (get) higher, I .... (call) the doctor.

f I .... (tell) you the big secret if .... (ask) me.

g If you .... (buy) that old picture, what .... you .... (do) with it?

More practice

Conditional type 1

ADVICE

You'll fail the exam if you don't study hard.

PREDICTION

If sea levels rise, many places will flood.

PROMISE

I'll do your homework for you if you buy me an ice cream.

THREAT

If you don't buy me an ice cream, I won't do your homework.

WARNING

If it rains this afternoon, you'll get soaking wet.

Remember ... after *if*, don't use the future (*will, be going to*, etc.).

I'll pass on your message if I will see him.

1 Write promises.

a If you ___lend___ (lend) me your phone, I ___'ll buy___ (buy) you supper!

b I _____ (help) with the cleaning if I _____ (get) there on time.

c I _____ (come) to the gym with you if you _____ (promise) not to eat chocolate for a month.

d If you _____ (change) your mind, we _____ (give) you a full refund.

e If you _____ (need) help with any difficult questions, I _____ (explain) them to you.

2 Write advice.

a If you ___watch___ (watch) this film, you ___'ll learn___ (learn) about the planets.

b You _____ (can) see the beach if you _____ (go) to that window.

c They _____ (send) you an information pack if you _____ (write) to them.

d Your tutor _____ (help) you if you _____ (ask).

e If you _____ (book) your flight early, you _____ (save) a lot of money.

f If you _____ (lock) the door, you _____ (be) much safer.

Wow! A holiday on Mars! Tickets are one billion dollars each!

Holiday on Mars!

I'm too old! I'm too poor! I'll never go to Mars ... but ...

This is a **past verb**, but the meaning isn't past. It's an **imaginary** time.

if I went, I'd take my sunglasses!

not totally impossible ... but unlikely!

= **I would**

She's imagining something that will probably never happen.

If you saw a fight, would you phone the police?

If I met my hero, I wouldn't ask for an autograph.

If Marcia needed help, she'd certainly ask.

If I didn't have a bike, I'd borrow Tom's.

past verb

I can't swim, but if I could, I'd go every week.

She can't swim. But she can imagine a different present.

I don't know the answer, but if I knew it, I wouldn't tell him!

We can reverse the order of the sentence parts. We don't use a comma.

> Would you phone the police if you saw a fight?

> I wouldn't ask for an autograph if I met my hero.

Both correct grammar
The meaning is different

Conditional type 1

> If you have a car, you'll get there in about ten minutes.

The speaker thinks it is **possible** that the person has a car.

(50% chance)

Conditional type 2

> If you had a car, you'd get there in about ten minutes.

The speaker thinks it is **unlikely** that the person has a car.

(0–10% chance)

1 Change Peter's sentences to show that he thinks these things are *unlikely* to happen.

a If I make a mistake, I'll tell you.
If I made a mistake, I'd tell you.

b If I get a job, I'll start saving.
....

c You'll pay less if you go to a bed and breakfast hotel.
....

d If our team loses to Portsmouth, we'll be out of the competition.
....

e We can get to the finals if we win against Barcelona.
....

f If everyone gives 10% of their income, we'll feed the whole world.
....

g If you find €100 in the street, will you report it to the police?
....

2 Make answers using conditional type 2.

a **Jeremy:** What's the answer to question 7?
Pauline: *If I knew, I'd tell you!*
(I / knew / I / tell / you)

b **Maria:** Eat that cake!
Rob: ....
(I / want / it / I / eat / it)

c **Brett:** Have you done your homework yet?
Wendy: ....
(I / understand / it / I / do / it)

d **Barbara:** Can I borrow $20?
Craig: ....
(I / have / some money / I / lend / it / you)

e **Andy:** Dawn! Dawn! There's a spider! There's a spider!
Dawn: ....
(I / believe / you / I / be / frightened!)

I can ... Ask about unlikely futures

Conditional type 2 • questions

> What would you do if you lost your job?

> What would you do if you got seriously ill?

> What would you do if she left you?

> What would you do if you needed money urgently?

> What would you do if someone stole your wallet?

> What would you do if you were me?

> What would you do if your computer crashed?

> What would you do if there was a fire?

What would you do / say / think / suggest / choose, etc. ... if ... + Past Simple

> Past Simple verb, but not a past meaning

> This refers to an imaginary future.

What would you do if your friend told you he cheated in an exam?

> It may or may not happen.

What would you say if I told you that I've resigned?
What would you think if I said 'No'?
What would you suggest if I asked your opinion?

We can also ask Where would you go if ...? Who would you call if ...?, etc.

Where would you go if you owned a luxury yacht?
Who would you call if you needed help?

---

1 Complete the sentences with the verbs in brackets in the correct form.

a What would you do if you ___lost___ (lose) a valuable piece of jewellery?

b What would you do if you _____ (become) President of the USA?

c What would you do if you _____ (win) $10,000?

d Where would you go if you _____ (have) a really fast car?

e What would you do if you _____ (be) stuck in an elevator?

f Who would you ask for help if you urgently _____ (need) a lot of money?

g What would you do if you _____ (discover) that you _____ (have) superhero powers?

h What would you do if your friend _____ (tell) you that he usually _____ (cheat) in exams?

2 You are the Chief Executive of a computer company. Ask your senior managers some questions with *What would you do / say / think / recommend if ...?*

a You think that profits might fall next year. (do)
What would you do if profits fell next year?

b You are worried that there might be a big earthquake. (do)

c You might reduce salaries by 10% next year. (think)

d You think that you might find a spy from a rival company. (say)

e You think you want to save $20 million. (recommend)

More practice

I can ... Give advice by saying what I would do

If I were you ...

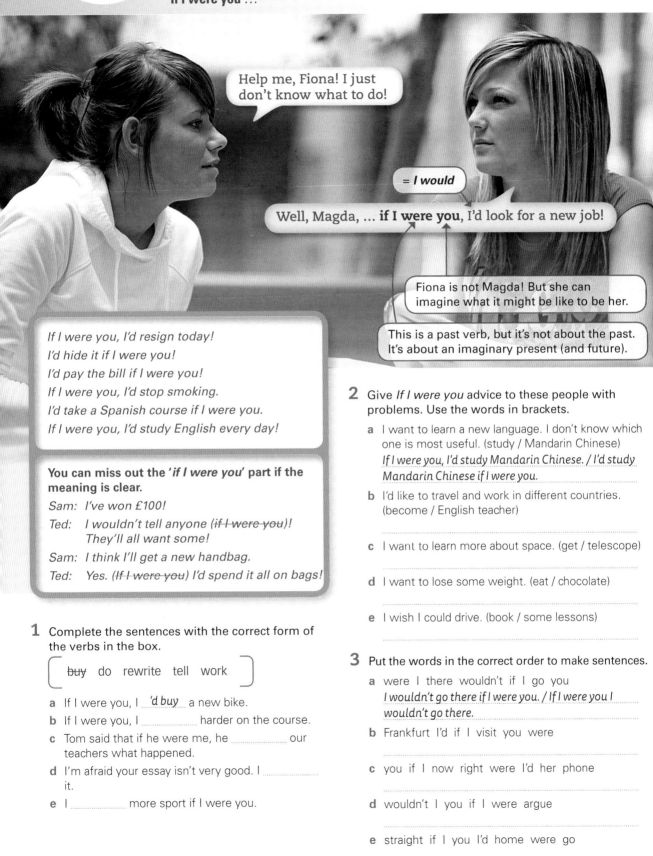

Help me, Fiona! I just don't know what to do!

= *I would*

Well, Magda, ... **if I were you**, I'd look for a new job!

Fiona is not Magda! But she can imagine what it might be like to be her.

This is a past verb, but it's not about the past. It's about an imaginary present (and future).

If I were you, I'd resign today!
I'd hide it if I were you!
I'd pay the bill if I were you!
If I were you, I'd stop smoking.
I'd take a Spanish course if I were you.
If I were you, I'd study English every day!

You can miss out the 'if I were you' part if the meaning is clear.

Sam: I've won £100!

Ted: I wouldn't tell anyone (if I were you)!
*   They'll all want some!*

Sam: I think I'll get a new handbag.

Ted: Yes. (If I were you) I'd spend it all on bags!

1 Complete the sentences with the correct form of the verbs in the box.

> ~~buy~~ do rewrite tell work

a If I were you, I ___'d buy___ a new bike.
b If I were you, I _____ harder on the course.
c Tom said that if he were me, he _____ our teachers what happened.
d I'm afraid your essay isn't very good. I _____ it.
e I _____ more sport if I were you.

2 Give *If I were you* advice to these people with problems. Use the words in brackets.

a I want to learn a new language. I don't know which one is most useful. (study / Mandarin Chinese)
   If I were you, I'd study Mandarin Chinese. / I'd study Mandarin Chinese if I were you.

b I'd like to travel and work in different countries. (become / English teacher)

c I want to learn more about space. (get / telescope)

d I want to lose some weight. (eat / chocolate)

e I wish I could drive. (book / some lessons)

3 Put the words in the correct order to make sentences.

a were I there wouldn't if I go you
   I wouldn't go there if I were you. / If I were you I wouldn't go there.

b Frankfurt I'd if I visit you were

c you if I now right were I'd her phone

d wouldn't I you if I were argue

e straight if I you I'd home were go

More practice

I can ... # Give people advice about specific problems

had better (not)

We're lost!

We'd better ask someone for dirctions.

Kay asked me to phone her at 7 o'clock. I'd better not forget!

I'm tired.

You'd better have a rest.

It's 5 o'clock. We'd better go home.

We're late.

We'd better phone Carla and tell her.

I fell in the mud!

You'd better walk on the path from now on!

There's a nasty looking bull in this field.

We'd better go a different way.

It's looking at us!

Then you'd better not make any loud noises!

We can use *had better / 'd better* to give strong advice to someone (or to myself) about a specific present or future situation. It has a similar meaning to *should*. When I say *You'd better speak to her now*, I'm saying that I believe that it is very important or necessary for you to speak to her.

When I use *had better*, I'm suggesting that something bad might happen if you don't follow my advice! I can imagine continuing the sentences with *or ...* and something negative.

You'd better get ready ... or we'll be late.

I'd better call my boss ... or he'll be very angry with me.

I/You/He/She/It/We/They	'd better / had better	tell you the truth.
		go home now.
		retake the exam.
		apologise as soon as possible.
		try harder.

 Don't use an infinitive with *to*.

✗ *You'd better ~~to~~ come with me.*

Make negatives with *'d better not*.

You'd better not tell anyone my secret!

I'd better not make a lot of noise.

 Although *had better* includes the word *had*, it is NOT a past tense. It is about the present or future, not the past.

 Although *had better* includes the word *better*, it is NOT a comparative.

1 Choose the best response for each situation.

The situation

a Someone rings your doorbell. You open the door and see that it's pouring with rain and your friend is soaking wet.

b You are a Maths teacher. One of your students has given you his answers to an exercise. You see that there are many careless mistakes.

c I don't want to hear the football results!

d Mike phones you. He says that when he came home, he found that his TV and games console were missing from his flat.

e You collect your seven-year-old daughter after school. She is crying. She says she had a fight with her best friend.

f I've eaten lots of cake and chocolate.

g Your mum says that she has a terrible backache.

h The radio says that there is a huge traffic jam on the road that your dad usually drives on to work.

You say …

1 You'd better see a doctor.

2 You'd better tell me all about it.

3 You'd better come in!

4 You'd better not listen to the news!

5 You'd better go a different way this morning.

6 You'd better check those again.

7 You'd better call the police.

8 You'd better not have any more!

2 Give some advice to these people using *had better (not)*. (Many different answers are possible.)

a 'I'm hungry.'

You'd better have some food.

b 'I'm tired.'

c 'I'm cold.'

d 'I'm bored.'

e 'I had a terrible argument with my dad.'

f 'I've got a headache.'

g 'I'm going to miss my bus!'

h 'I've left my lunch at home!'

i 'I forgot to phone Sam this morning!'

I can ... Say how I am prepared for possible events

in case + Present Simple, **in case of** + noun, **just in case**

> I don't like this hotel. It's a scary part of town! Do you think it's safe to go out?

> Hmm. Well, you have to be careful.

> Take a map **in case** you get lost.

> Have you got my phone number **in case** you need to call me?

> Don't hold your phone in your hand **in case** someone tries to steal it.

> **In case of** emergency, dial 911.

> Remember – we've got holiday insurance. **Just in case**.

in case tells about preparation for a possible event but ... we do not know if the event will happen or not. Often we are preparing for possible problems or bad situations.

Please | wear a tie | in case | we meet any VIPs!

[preparation for a possible event]   [an event that may or may not happen]

	in case	+ subject	+ Present Simple verb phrase
I'm taking £100		I	need money later today.
Take a dictionary		you	don't understand the lecture.
Take some food		you	feel hungry.
Let's go to the station early	*in case*	the train	is full.
Watch the patient carefully		he	gets worse.
Take a raincoat		it	rains.
I've made a space in my diary		we	need to have a meeting.
Josie's made lots of food		everyone	comes tonight.

in case is not the same as *if*.

Put on your raincoat in case it starts to rain. (= put on your raincoat because it might rain later).

Put on your raincoat if it starts to rain. (= put on your raincoat after it starts to rain).

We can also use *in case of* + noun. This means 'if there is'. You often see this on notices.

IN CASE OF EMERGENCY Dial 112 ← = if there is an emergency

In case of fire, do not use the lifts. ← = if there is a fire

in case of	noun	
	fire	problems
in case of	emergency	difficulty
	an accident	trouble

We can say *just in case* to mean that we are preparing for something that might happen (but we don't give a detailed explanation).

I'm going to take my passport, just in case.

'Why have you saved so much money?' 'Oh. You know! Just in case!'

1 Match the sentence beginnings with the endings.

a Take some aspirin with you
b Freia will translate everything at the presentation
c I'm going to buy my plane tickets tonight
d Please phone the Duty Manager on extension 73
e There will be bottles of water every kilometre
f The answers are at the back of the book

1 in case they get more expensive next week.
2 in case any of the runners need them.
3 in case you get a headache.
4 in case you can't work them out on your own.
5 in case some of the guests don't speak Finnish.
6 in case of emergency.

2 Say how you will prepare for some possible situations. (Many different answers are possible.)

a The weather forecast says it may be very sunny today.

I'll take some sun cream in case it's very sunny.

b The weather forecast says it may be rainy today.

c The news says that there might be a transport strike tomorrow.

d You are cooking steak for seven guests tonight. But you are not sure if any of them are vegetarian.

e You are worried that your alarm will not ring tomorrow morning and you'll be late for your exam.

f You want to watch *Celebrity Shoes* on TV at 7 p.m. But you think you might not get home till 8.30.

3 Which notice should go on the wall in each cartoon?

a In case of small fire, break glass
b In case of boredom, break glass
c In case of extreme hunger, break glass

Present Simple passive

So, let me just check I understand what a typical day is like ...

The building's **unlocked** at 5.30 a.m.

The alarm **is turned off** then, of course.

The factory floor **is cleaned**.

The machinery **is checked** and **switched on**.

The front doors **are opened** at 8.30.

The production line **is operated** from 9 to 7.

Everything **is switched off** at 7.30.

Lunch **is served** in two shifts at 12.30 and 1.15.

The factory **is closed** after everyone has left.

We don't know who did these things.
OR
We aren't interested in who did these things.
OR
It's not important who did these things.

We are interested in what was done ... not the people who did them.

Active:	She prints the weekly report on Tuesdays.	The HR department takes photos of every new employee.	They give certificates to all the winners.
Passive:	The weekly report is printed on Tuesdays.	Photos are taken of every new employee.	Certificates are given to all the winners.

Statement	Negative	Questions
The building's unlocked at 5.30 a.m.	The building isn't unlocked at 5.30 a.m.	Is the building unlocked at 5.30 a.m?
		When is the building unlocked?

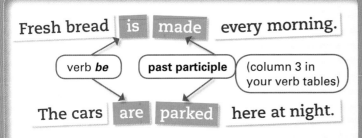

Fresh bread **is** **made** every morning.

verb *be* — past participle — (column 3 in your verb tables)

The cars **are** **parked** here at night.

If an object is *made of* something, it still looks like that material.

It's made of plastic.

These toys are made of wood.

If an object is *made from* something, it has usually changed into something different.

These toys are made from local trees. **(i.e. They are not trees any more – they are toys!)**

This juice is made from the finest fruit. **(i.e. It isn't fruit any more – it's juice!)**

We can also use *made with* to name ingredients or contents.

This pancake is made with local eggs.

1 Complete the sentences with the Present Simple passive form of the verbs in brackets.

a The storeroom _is locked_ (lock) at nine o'clock every night.

b Your certificate .... (print) on high quality paper.

c The advertisements .... (design) very carefully.

d The liquid .... (store) in these barrels.

e Only these three computers .... (connect) to the internet.

f Dinner .... (serve) in the upstairs dining room.

g The music .... (record) in this studio.

h This bridge .... (repaint) every 12 months.

2 Complete the sentences about the daily life of a shopping centre. Use the verbs in the box in the Present Simple passive.

> ask clean close lock
> make open staff ~~test~~

a The fire alarms _are tested_ every morning at 7.00 a.m.

b All the floors of the shopping centre .... before any customers arrive.

c The doors .... at 8.30 a.m. and the public come in.

d The information desk .... between 9.00 a.m. and 7.00 p.m.

e Announcements .... on the loudspeakers during the day.

f At 7.50 p.m. everyone .... to leave.

g The centre .... and .... at 8.15 p.m.

3 *INTERNET* QUIZ

What are these things made from? Use the internet to help you.

a Waffles
b Most dolls
c Chocolate
d Glass
e Marmalade
f Yoghurt
g Birds' nests

1 is made from cocoa beans and sugar.
2 is made from oranges and sugar.
3 are made from wheat flour, baking powder, eggs and milk.
4 are usually made from sticks and twigs.
5 is made from milk.
6 are made of plastic.
7 is made from sand and other minerals.

4 Make two new sentences like exercise 3.

a .... made ....
b .... made ....

I can ... Talk about historical facts

Past Simple passive

Anna Karenina **was written** by Tolstoy.

The Pyramids **were built** on the banks of the Nile.

The electric light bulb **was invented** in 1879.

Oil **was discovered** in Saudi Arabia in the 1930s.

The first ever plane **was flown** on a windy beach in North Carolina, USA.

The Olympics **were held** in London in 2012.

Julius Caesar **was killed** by his friend Brutus.

Active	Tolstoy wrote Anna Karenina.	Brutus killed Julius Caesar.	Great Britain held the Olympics in London in 2012. *
Passive	Anna Karenina *was written* by Tolstoy.	Julius Caesar was killed by Brutus.	The Olympics were held in London in 2012.

* Sometimes you need to add a subject (e.g. Great Britain) to make an active sentence!

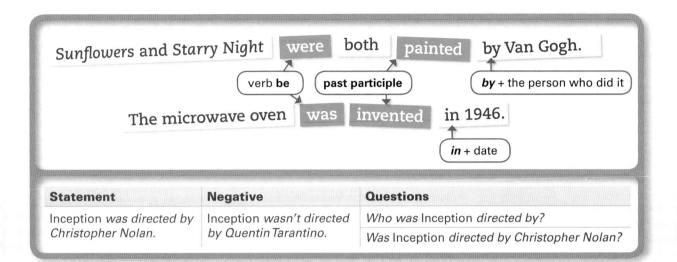

Sunflowers and Starry Night **were** both **painted** by Van Gogh.

verb **be**   past participle   **by** + the person who did it

The microwave oven **was** **invented** in 1946.

in + date

Statement	Negative	Questions
Inception *was directed by Christopher Nolan.*	Inception *wasn't directed by Quentin Tarantino.*	*Who was* Inception *directed by?*
		Was Inception *directed by Christopher Nolan?*

1 INTERNET QUIZ 🔍

Make correct sentences. Check the internet if you need help!

a The film *Shutter Island* — was discovered by — Bob Kane.
b The novel *Pride and Prejudice* — was written by — 2010.
c The inside of the Statue of Liberty — was created by — Martin Scorsese.
d The character of Batman — was directed by — 1066.
e Penicillin — was invaded in — Jane Austen.
f The first iPad — was designed by — Alexander Fleming.
g England — was launched in — Gustave Eiffel.

2
Use the words to make questions with the Past Simple passive.

a When / President Kennedy / assassinate
When was President Kennedy assassinated?

b When / the first Barbie doll / make

c Where / the first Olympic Games / hold

d Which film / award / the 'Best Picture' Oscar / in 2012

e When / the first mobile phone / demonstrate

f Where / *The Lord of the Rings* and *The Hobbit* / film

g When / the first tweet / send

h What / discover / in Egypt / in 1922

3 INTERNET QUIZ 🔍

Here are the answers to the questions in exercise 2. Can you match them with the questions? Use the internet to help you.

> 1959 1963 1973 2006 Greece
> New Zealand *The Artist* Tutankhamen's tomb

4
Complete the story with the verbs in brackets in the Past Simple passive.

The Berlin Wall

A long wall used to divide the German city of Berlin. Some western visitors *were allowed* [a] (allow) to visit East Berlin, but very few East Berlin citizens .... [b] (give) permission to leave. At the border, each passport .... [c] (check) carefully and many people .... [d] (search). Some brave East Berliners tried to escape in various ways, but many .... [e] (catch) and some .... [f] (shoot). Everything changed in 1989. On one amazing evening, the barriers .... [g] (open) and thousands of people went through the checkpoints. Celebrations .... [h] (hold) all over the city. Soon after, the hated wall .... [i] (pull down) and, before long, the whole of Germany .... [j] (reunite).

> Has the agenda **been printed?**

> Have all the managers **been invited?**

> Has lunch **been ordered?**

> Has the projector **been tested?**

> Has the air conditioning **been repaired?**

She isn't interested in <u>who</u> did these things. She just wants to know if they have been done ... so that they are ready <u>now</u>.

Active	*Have you printed the agenda?*	*Has George ordered lunch?*	*Have they tested the projector?*
Passive	*Has the agenda been printed?*	*Has lunch been ordered?*	*Has the projector been tested?*

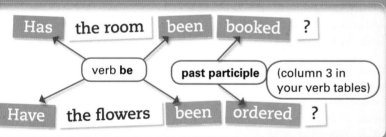

| **Has** | the room | **been** | **booked** | ? |

verb **be** — past participle (column 3 in your verb tables)

| **Have** | the flowers | **been** | **ordered** | ? |

Statement
The agenda has been sent.

Negative
The agenda hasn't been sent.

Question
Has the agenda been sent?

Short answers
Yes, it has. No, it hasn't.

---

1 Julie's new café opens today. Mark's new theatre opens tonight. Who said each of these questions – Julie or Mark?

a Has the kitchen been cleaned? ...*Julie*...

b Have all the tickets been sold? ....

c Have the tables been laid? ....

d Have enough fresh vegetables been bought?
....

e Has the fake gun been tested? ....

f Have photos of the stars been put up outside the building? ....

g Has the fridge been repaired? ....

h Have all the waiters been trained? ....

2 Kate is getting ready for a birthday party. Complete her questions with the words in the box in the correct form.

> ~~clean~~ decorate put up send
> tell turn on wash wrap

a Has the room *been cleaned* ?

b Have all the plates .... ?

c Have the presents .... ?

d Have the decorations .... ?

e Has the oven .... ?

f Has the cake .... ?

g Have the children .... to bed?

h Has the DJ .... where to go?

More practice

Present Perfect passive and Past Simple passive

Mum ... the drink's been spilt on the floor.

I don't want to say that it was me!

The liquid was poured into the test tube.

The scientific facts are important. It doesn't matter who did it.

The TV's been stolen!

We don't know who did it.

Don't worry. The problem has been solved.

I'm too modest to say that I solved it!

Use *by* if you do want to say who did the action.
Your new camera has been broken by those children.

1 Rewrite the sentences so that the person (or people) who did the action is not mentioned.

a The boss gave Jedd a new job.
Jedd was given a new job.

b Mike's secretary has lost the report.

c The children have tidied the room.

d The dogs tore the newspapers.

e Some thieves have stolen the jewellery.

f The people elected Mark Andrews.

g The company has sacked Pat.

h The party guests ate all the food.

i Some noisy protestors have interrupted the lecture.

2 Complete the Past Simple passive sentences with the verbs in brackets. Add *by* to each sentence and ideas from the box.

> my mother   my two-year-old daughter   our local team
> the local newspaper   the managing directors   ~~the police~~

a The vandals (arrest) *The vandals were arrested by the police.*

b The story (print)

c This picture (draw)

d These suggestions (make)

e These cakes (bake)

f These football cups (win)

3 Jacqui is doing a live scientific experiment on the internet. Change her sentences into the Present Perfect passive.

a I've placed the equipment on the table.
The equipment has been placed on the table.

b Colin has collected the chemicals from the fridge.

c Teresa has shut the windows and she has switched off the lights.

d Viewers have asked lots of questions on the blog.

e Scientists have never found an answer for this problem.

 I can ...

Talk about something unexpected that happened

Past Simple passive with **got**

Last night, Andy got followed home from the club.

He got chased through the old town.

They got stopped by ... a ... superhero!

They both got caught.

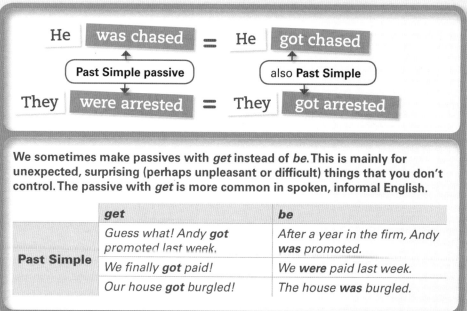

| He | was chased | = | He | got chased |

Past Simple passive

also **Past Simple**

| They | were arrested | = | They | got arrested |

We sometimes make passives with *get* instead of *be*. This is mainly for unexpected, surprising (perhaps unpleasant or difficult) things that you don't control. The passive with *get* is more common in spoken, informal English.

	get	**be**
Past Simple	Guess what! Andy **got** promoted last week.	After a year in the firm, Andy **was** promoted.
	We finally **got** paid!	We **were** paid last week.
	Our house **got** burgled!	The house **was** burgled.

> *Get* can be used with the passive to emphasise the action. For example, *The window was broken* could refer to a state (a window that is already broken) OR an action (somebody breaking a window), but *The window got broken* refers to the action (somebody breaking a window). Other examples:
>
> The whole area **got** flooded.
>
> The painting **got** stolen.
>
> The car **got** damaged.

1 Look at the pictures and say what happened to the people. Use the verbs in the box in the correct form.

> ~~catch~~   flood   leave behind   lose   mix up   pay

a

Luckily, the muggers *got caught.*

b

Unfortunately, the tourists ....

c

Mary's keys ....

d

The two suitcases ....

e

Their home ....

f

Last Friday, I ....

2 You've just come back from a terrible holiday! Tell your friends all the bad things that happened to you.

a Your flight was delayed by 24 hours.
Our *flight got delayed by 24 hours.*

b They transferred you to a worse hotel.
We *got transferred to a worse hotel.*

c Someone invited you to a terrible party.
We ....

d The police arrested you.
We ....

e They released you six hours later!
We ....

f They asked Jorge for some money.
Jorge ....

g They cancelled your flight back!
Our ....

h They sent your luggage to the wrong airport.
Our ....

Overview of passives

In a passive sentence, the object becomes the new subject!

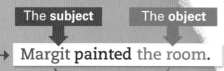

The **subject**   The **object**

Active → Margit painted the room.

Passive → The room was painted.

No object!

We could add 'by Margit' if we want to say who did the action.

To form the passive, use *be* (in the correct tense) and the past participle.

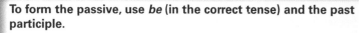

Present Simple	is	made
Present Progressive	is being	painted
Present Perfect	has been	built
Past Simple	was	taken
Past Progressive	was being	flooded
will future	will be	designed
be going to	is going to be	sold

Present

	Active	Passive
Simple	she cooks pizza	pizza is cooked
Progressive	she is cooking pizza	pizza is being cooked
Perfect	she has cooked pizza	pizza has been cooked

Past

	Active	Passive
Simple	she cooked pizza	pizza was cooked
Progressive	she was cooking pizza	pizza was being cooked

Future

	Active	Passive
will	she will cook pizza	pizza will be cooked
be going to	she is going to cook pizza	pizza is going to be cooked

Use the passive:

- **to describe processes and routines (manufacture, science, agriculture, etc.)**
  e.g. *The wheat is harvested in June.*

- **when you want to sound formal (in written reports, etc.)**
  e.g. *The chemicals were mixed and stirred.*

- **when you don't want to say who did something (in academic papers, etc.)**
  e.g. *The wrong decision was made.*

- **when you don't know who did something (a crime, an accident, etc.)**
  e.g. *The fence has been broken.*

- **when you want to focus on what is done (not the doer)**
  e.g. *The witness was warned to tell the truth.*

1 Put the words in the correct order to make sentences.

a has found been cat Mia's
Mia's cat has been found.

b changed the been has password

c lunch prepared being is

d sent will exam be the week next results

e the repaired being alarm was

f properly the closed wasn't gate

g going cancelled the is to be wedding

2 Each passive sentence has one mistake (one wrong word or one missing word). Correct the mistakes.

a ~~The game has be stopped.~~
The game has been stopped.

b The boat was steal after midnight.

c The concert hall going to be redecorated next month.

d The DVD player and the TV was broken.

e The customer's order is been packed in those large boxes over there.

f Don't panic! The missing tiger will be find!

g The essays were be marked in the staff room.

h That film will never be show in our country.

3 Answer these questions with the Present or Past Progressive passive.

a Why can't we go into the museum? (repair)
It's being repaired.

b Why couldn't you go to the museum yesterday? (decorate)
It was being decorated.

c Why can't I wear my new shirt? (wash)

d Why couldn't I see their new baby boy? (change)

e Why can't we have lunch now? (cook)

f Why couldn't we borrow the plates and glasses last night? (use)

g Why can't the actors take a lunch break? (film)

h Why couldn't the soldiers escape back to camp? (attack)

4 Change each sentence into the passive. Then decide <u>why</u> the speaker used the passive. Is Reason (i) or Reason (ii) more likely?
Reason (i) to avoid blame
Reason (ii) not knowing who did/will do it

a Dad, I've spilt the juice.
Dad, the juice has been spilt. Reason (i)

b Someone has stolen our TV!

c I gave that tourist the wrong information.

d People sprayed graffiti on the old fountain.

e Some people will clean the office after the party.

f We were playing heavy metal music much too loud.

g Strangers are going to interrupt the Minister's speech.

h Some people searched them at the airport.

had in different structures

Some words in English can be VERY confusing. 'Had' is definitely one of them!

1 We **had** lunch at the station café.

> Main verb **have** in the Past Simple.

2 They **had** been there many times before.

> Auxiliary verb used to help make the Past Perfect tense.

3 I had **had** too many coffees!

> Past participle of **have** used in the Present Perfect and Past Perfect.

'd (= would) and *'d (=had)* are often mixed up!

I'd like a milkshake, please. → **would**

She'd never eaten cucumber sandwiches before. → **had**

Common examples of *'d = would*:
'd like   'd love   'd hate   'd prefer
'd rather   'd be

---

1 Decide whether *had* is used like 1, 2 or 3 in the explanations above.

a The children had too much cake at the party and they all felt ill.   *1*

b Have the directors had their afternoon break yet?   ....

c Had the directors finished their meeting?   ....

d Kate had cleaned the old curtains.   ....

e Kate had old curtains.   ....

f Kate had washed the old curtains.   ....

2 Use the words to write some new sentences like 1, 2 and 3.

a Teresa green hat repair
1 *Teresa had a green hat.*
2 *Teresa had repaired a green hat.*
3 *Teresa had had a green hat.*

b The actors new costumes make
1 ....
2 ....
3 ....

c Marina three magazines deliver
1 ....
2 ....
3 ....

d Susie expensive black shoes clean
1 ....
2 ....
3 ....

3 Use the word pool to:

a make three sentences with the main verb *have*.
1 *Anne had a new printer.*
2 ....
3 ....

b make three Past Perfect sentences.
1 *Anne had finished her report.*
2 ....
3 ....

Anne   had   finished   a
lunch   printed   checked   the
report   made   her
boss   printer   repaired   new

4 In each sentence, decide whether *'d* means *would* or *had*.

a We'd love to see some photos of your new baby.   *would*

b I'd hate to make any problems.   ....

c He'd hated broccoli all his life.   ....

d She'd like to play football.   ....

e She said she'd play football.   ....

f She said she'd played football.   ....

g They'd been to the cinema.   ....

h I'd be so happy!   ....

More practice

Reflexive pronouns (1)

Enjoy **yourselves**!

Help **yourself**.

I bought **myself** a cowboy hat!

Oh, no. My cowboy shot **himself**!

And I got **myself** a present! Look! A new scarf!

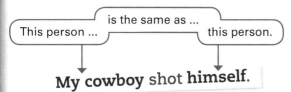

Use reflexive pronouns when ...

the person or people who do the action are the same as the person or people it's done to!

This person ... is the same as ... this person.

My cowboy shot himself.

Singular		Plural	
I did it	myself	We did it	ourselves
You did it	yourself	You did it	yourselves
He did it	himself	They did it	themselves
She did it	herself		
It did it	itself		

Help yourself! = Take whatever you want!

I enjoyed myself. = I had a good time.

Let yourself in. = You can unlock or open the door yourself. You don't need to wait for someone else.

⚠️ **Don't use with:** f~~ee~~l

I feel ~~myself~~ very comfortable here. → *I feel very comfortable here.*

---

1 Complete the sentences using the correct reflexive pronoun.

a Our baby son was so tired last night. He cried _himself_ to sleep.

b My little sister is too young to look after ....

c I hope our cousins behave ....

d Come in, Judy! It's so good you could come. Make .... comfortable. Would you like a drink?

e We made .... some lunch.

2 Complete the sentences. Use a verb from the box and a reflexive pronoun.

> blame enjoy help let look
> ~~see~~ set teach throw

a The young children screamed when they _saw themselves_ in the strange mirror.

b The princess .... at .... in the mirror and said the magic words.

c Did the guests .... at the wedding party?

d There's nothing left! I think the children came in and .... to all the cakes!

e If there's no one at home when you arrive you can .... in.

f I wanted to speak to local people so I .... Russian before I went to Moscow.

g I wanted to warn Joe about the broken ladder – but I completely forgot. I .... for the accident.

h If you want to do well in sport, you must .... targets.

i Your brother's very angry! He just ran into the house and .... onto his bed.

Say that someone did something (and not another person)

Reflexive pronouns (2)

Did you help her?

No, she did it **herself**!

Can I help with the ironing?

I've already done it all **myself**!

The door closed by **itself**!

The statues are moving by **themselves**!

Your room is a terrible mess.

Don't worry! We'll tidy it **ourselves**.

> **We can use reflexive pronouns if we want to emphasise that someone did something.**
>
> That's a great report. Did George and other people in the office help you?
>
> No! I wrote it <u>myself</u>!
>
> ME! Not George! Not other people! ME! ME! ME!

> **by + reflexive pronoun = without any help**
> *I recorded the whole song by myself.* **= It was only me, alone – no one else!**

1 Complete the sentences using phrases from the box.

> bought it myself!   broke it myself
> found it myself!   ~~paid for it myself~~
> scored it myself   wrote it all by myself

a My mum didn't lend me the money to buy my new car! I .*paid for it myself!*.......

b My boss didn't help me with that report!
I ....

c I lied! It wasn't a dog that smashed the vase. Sorry,
I ....

d Look at this beautiful rock crystal.
I ....

e Michael didn't score that goal!
I ....

f Peter didn't get that present for Francis.
I ....

2 Complete the sentences with the correct pronoun.

a 'I can help you look for the CD.'
'Don't worry! I found it ...*myself.*... '

b 'There were so many mistakes in Nick's essay.'
'Don't worry! He's already corrected them all
....

c 'Shall I give Ian his security badge?'
'Don't worry! I've already given it to him
....

d 'I think we should help them to launch the boat.'
'Don't worry. They've already done it ....

e 'They all went home. The work is only half-finished!'
'Don't worry. We can finish it ....

f Listen, children! Don't ask people to help you with this task. I want you to do it all by ....

More practice

must be, can't be

> We've been chatting for ages! Oh – look outside! It's dark already! It **must be** after 8 o'clock!

> Hey! Someone's left their phone here! Whose is it?

> Hmm. It's not mine. And it **can't be** Diana's because she took her phone with her.

> It's quite old. It **must be** Jackie's. She has an old phone and she was in this office about half an hour ago.

We use *must be* and *can't be* when we are guessing the answer to something we don't know. We are not 100% certain (and our conclusions might be wrong).

We use *must be* when we think about all the facts we know and try to decide what we believe is true.

Can't be is the negative of *must be*. We use it when we believe that it is <u>not</u> possible that something is true.

Facts I know	My guess
The phone is old.	*It must be Jackie's phone.*
Jackie has an old phone.	
Jackie was here half an hour ago.	*It can't be Diana's phone.*
We've been talking for a long time.	*It must be after 8 o'clock.*
It's dark outside.	

> ! Remember – these things are not definitely correct. They are guesses and may be wrong!

1 Read Sophia's comments. Write Ben's reply using *must be* and the word in brackets.

a Sophia: What?!? My electricity bill says $20,000,034.02!

Ben: (mistake)
It must be a mistake!

b Sophia: There was a strange noise in the cellar and all the lights went out!

Ben: (ghost) Ha ha!

c Sophia: Oh no! The poster for this film has spaceships and robots on it!

Ben: (sci-fi film)

d Sophia: Hey! My lunch box hasn't got any food in it – just pictures of bread!

Ben: (joke)

e Sophia: That man's asking lots of questions about what happened last Saturday.

Ben: (detective)

2 Read the facts. Choose one or more possible conclusions. Cross out the unlikely conclusions.

Facts

a I've lost my keys.
They're not in my pocket.
I usually put them on the kitchen table, on top of the TV or in my desk.
The keys are not on the kitchen table.
The keys are not on top of the TV.

Conclusions

~~They must be on the kitchen table.~~
~~They must be in my pocket.~~
They must be in my desk. ✓
~~They can't be in my desk.~~

b Someone is ringing the doorbell.
Mike isn't here this week. He's in Bolivia.
Susan called me an hour ago. She said she was walking to our house.
Lou likes visiting our house. He said he might come tomorrow.

It must be Susan.
It can't be Susan.
It must be Mike.
It can't be Mike.
It must be Lou.

c Every student passed the end of year exam with high marks.
All the students asked to have the same teacher next course.
There is always a lot of laughter in her classroom.

She can't be a good teacher.
She must be a good teacher.
She must be a bad teacher.
She must be a noisy teacher.

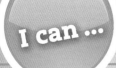

I can ... Talk about things that are necessary to do

have to, must, need to

> Are you really going to a boarding school* now?

> *a school where you live, eat, sleep, etc. in the school (and don't go home every day!)

> Yes! It's really different from my old school. We **have to** get up at 7.30 and we **have to** wear school uniform all the time.

> Yes, there are hundreds. Everyone **has to** follow all the rules.

> Are there a lot of rules?

> What happens if you break a rule?

> You **have to** run round the fields three times! Hey! It's 4 o'clock! I **have to** go! I **must** call my mum. Then I **need to** get ready for football! Let's talk tomorrow. And you **must** come and visit me here one day!

Must and *have to* have a very similar meaning. They mean that something is necessary or important to do.

I/you/we/they	have to	wait
	must	
he/she/it	has to	
	must	

Must and *have to* are often used differently.

Do I feel that **someone else** (e.g. parent, teacher, school, government) thinks it is necessary or important to do?	yes➡		*I have to tidy my room.*
Is it a law, rule, other person's order, etc?	yes➡	**have to**	*We have to pay income tax.*
Is it something I don't want to do?	yes➡		*I have to spend a whole day with my boring cousin.*
Is there an adverb of frequency?	yes➡		*The children usually have to go to bed at nine o'clock.*
Do I feel that something is important to do?	yes➡		*I must finish this game.*
Is it something I want to do?	yes➡	**must**	*I must talk to Sally about the film.*
Do I want to give friendly advice or a suggestion to someone?	yes➡		*You must try my soup!*

(with **no** arrow down the left side from the first question)

If you're talking and you are not sure whether to use *have to* or *must*, use *have to*. It's usually OK!

Need to has a similar meaning to **have to**

We need to buy more potatoes.

but it's not so common in positive sentences. It's most often used in the negative to say that something is not necessary or not important to do. See Unit 85.

You don't need to finish your homework now.

We usually use *have to* or *need to* (not *must*) in questions.

Do you have to go now?

Do you need to finish before six o'clock?

must →
- future ✓ *I must visit him next week.*
- present ✓ *I must finish my homework.*
- past ✗

have to →
- future ✓ *I have to call her on Tuesday.*
- present ✓ *I have to cook this meal.*
- past ✓ *I had to go home early.*

need to →
- future ✓ *I need to go there tomorrow.*
- present ✓ *I need to watch this programme.*
- past ✓ *I needed to take the test again.*

---

1 Match Pete's comments with the most likely replies from Sandra.

a I don't want to go to the party.
b Why are you leaving so early?
c Every time I try to make mayonnaise it goes wrong.
d Why did she drive them to the station?
e Were you feeling ill this morning?
f Did you fail your test?

1 I have to do some work for my parents.
2 They were late and had to rush for their train.
3 Oh, you must come! It'll be great!
4 Yes. I had to lie down and take some tablets.
5 I did! I need to study harder next time!
6 You need to add the oil very slowly and stir all the time.

2 Read the phone conversations and choose the correct verbs. Be careful: in some questions BOTH options are possible!

Conversation 1

Audrey: Hello, Andy. It's me. I'm on a business trip – but it's a disaster!

Andy: What happened?

Audrey: Well, it started at the airport. Our first plane broke down and they said we all ª *need to* ✗ / *had to* ✓ get off. So – oh, just a minute, Andy … I ᵇ *need to* ✓ / *have to* ✓ speak to someone here. I'll call you back in five minutes.

Conversation 2

Audrey: Hi, Andy! Me again! So … we finally took off five hours late. But the weather in Portugal was stormy and we ᶜ *had to* ...... / *must* ...... land at the wrong airport.

Andy: Are you there now?

Audrey: Yes. Listen, Andy – I ᵈ *have to* ...... / *need to* ...... call the factory in Lisbon, but I can't find the number. Can you help? You ᵉ *need to* ...... / *must* ...... phone them and apologise for us. Oh dear. Someone is telling us that we ᶠ *have to* ...... / *had to* ...... move away from this area. I'll call you again later.

3 Complete the sentences with *have to* in the correct form.

a I don't want to visit my aunt today – but my mum says I .*have to*. go.

b Mrs Stone is very sorry, but she .... cancel the meeting for next Tuesday.

c You .... try this apple pie! It's absolutely delicious!

d Luisa's not at home today because she .... go back to school this morning.

e Please tell the students that they .... wait here. They can't go into the exam room yet.

f Oh no! Asad has forgotten his packed lunch. .... we .... go back and collect it?

g Sit down, children! Don't run around! .... you .... make so much noise?

4 Look back at **3**. Choose four sentences where *must* would be a good alternative answer.

Must is a good alternative in

a ....*3a*....

b ....

c ....

d ....

I can ... **Talk about things that it is important not to do**

mustn't

> Yes – our charity has had a bad year. But we **mustn't** be negative.

> We **mustn't** stop our important work.

> We **mustn't** forget the important job we are doing.

> Our supporters **mustn't** lose their trust in us.

> We **mustn't** give up!

---

must not = mustn't

must = it is necessary or important that you **do** something

mustn't = it is necessary or important that you do **not** do something

We must all work harder = it is important that we all work harder.

We mustn't relax = it is important that we do NOT relax.

We often use *mustn't / must not* to talk about things it is necessary not to do because there are rules, regulations, laws, etc.

You mustn't smoke anywhere inside the college buildings.

Students must not park in the school car park.

You mustn't tell anyone your password.

Candidates must not talk at any time during the exam.

When *mustn't* has this meaning, the opposite is *can*:

You can smoke inside the college buildings.

Students can park in the school car park.

---

1 What are the things you *mustn't* do in your school? Decide if each sentence is true or false. If it's false, make a true sentence with *can*. (Different answers are possible.)

a You mustn't be rude to the teacher.   True / ~~False~~

b You mustn't eat food in the classroom. ~~True~~ / False
   You can eat food in the classroom.

c Teachers mustn't smoke in class.   True / False
   ....

d Parents mustn't phone the school.   True / False
   ....

e Students mustn't talk during written exams.
                                        True / False
   ....

f You mustn't take a holiday during term time.
                                        True / False
   ....

2 Tim is talking to himself. Complete his sentences with *mustn't* + a verb.

a Last year I forgot Jane's birthday! I .*mustn't forget*.
   it this year!

b Last week I forgot to do my English homework. I
   .... it this week!

c I failed the Physics exam last term. I
   .... this time.

d Last night I stayed out until 2 a.m. I
   .... out late again tonight!

e Yesterday I lost my car keys. It took twenty minutes
   to find them! I .... them again today!

f Yesterday I broke two of Sally's favourite cups! I
   .... any more today!

More practice

don't have to, don't need to

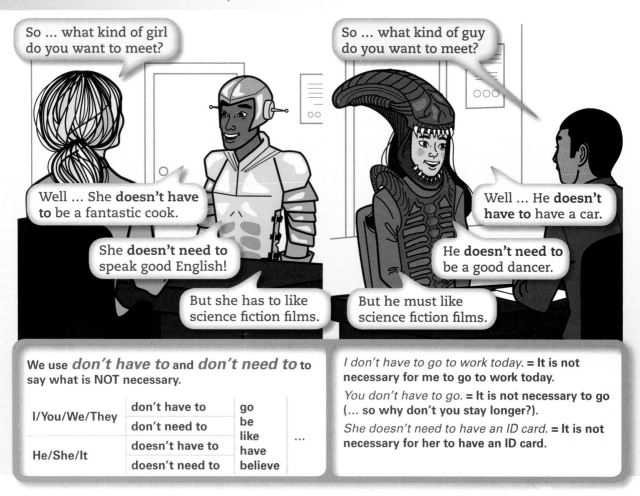

So ... what kind of girl do you want to meet?

Well ... She **doesn't have to** be a fantastic cook.

She **doesn't need to** speak good English!

But she has to like science fiction films.

So ... what kind of guy do you want to meet?

Well ... He **doesn't have to** have a car.

He **doesn't need to** be a good dancer.

But he must like science fiction films.

We use *don't have to* and *don't need to* to say what is NOT necessary.

I/You/We/They	don't have to	go
	don't need to	be
He/She/It	doesn't have to	like ... have
	doesn't need to	believe

I don't have to go to work today. **= It is not necessary for me to go to work today.**

You don't have to go. **= It is not necessary to go (... so why don't you stay longer?).**

She doesn't need to have an ID card. **= It is not necessary for her to have an ID card.**

---

1 Complete the sentences using *You don't have to ...* and a phrase from the box.

> apologise   come earlier   decide now
> ~~go yet~~   pay anything   pay in cash
> re-enter your password

a It's not late. *You don't have to go yet.* Stay a bit longer!

b Just go in! .... There's no entrance fee.

c Come at 10 o'clock. .... That would be a good time to start work.

d There's no hurry. .... You can tell me your decision tomorrow.

e Don't worry if you've left your money at home. .... You can use a credit card instead.

f You can get your email by clicking this button. .... The computer remembers it.

g It's OK! .... I wasn't upset by what you said! Really!

2 A tourist guide in New York is giving you advice about visiting the United Nations building. Underline the correct verb.

a You *mustn't* / *don't have to* be over 15 years old. The UN offers tours for adults and children.

b On Mondays to Fridays you must buy an advance guided tour ticket, but on Saturdays and Sundays you *mustn't* / *don't have to* book a ticket in advance to see the Visitor Centre. There is free walk-in access at 43rd Street.

c Unguided visits are not permitted. You *mustn't* / *don't have to* wander round on your own.

d You *don't have to* / *mustn't* speak English. Tours are offered in many other languages.

e Formal clothes must be worn in the Delegates' Dining Room. You *mustn't* / *don't have to* wear jeans.

f Of course, you *mustn't* / *don't have to* carry any knives or guns with you in the UN buildings.

g Visitors *don't have to* / *mustn't* buy anything in the shop – but you will probably want to take home a souvenir.

Talk about past actions that weren't necessary

needn't have, didn't need to

Molly is staying at her best friend Denise's flat. She woke up early this morning.

Oh, Molly! You're my guest! You **needn't have** washed the dishes!

Molly woke up.

Molly washed the dishes.

Denise woke up.

Denise saw the clean plates.

I know. I **didn't need to** do it! But I wanted to help!

7.10   7.40   8.10   8.40   now

She **did** the washing up. It was not necessary for her to do it.

She needn't have done the washing up.

She didn't need to do the washing up.

Anne and Karim are driving on the motorway.

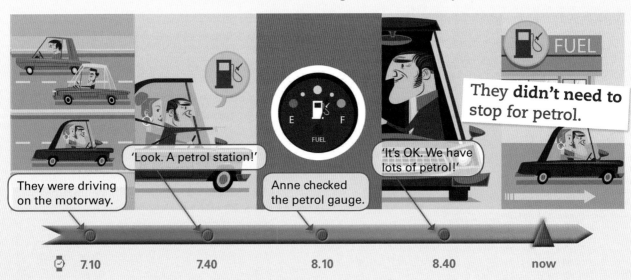

FUEL

They **didn't need to** stop for petrol.

They were driving on the motorway.

'Look. A petrol station!'

Anne checked the petrol gauge.

'It's OK. We have lots of petrol!'

7.10   7.40   8.10   8.40   now

They **didn't** stop for petrol. It was not necessary to stop.

They **didn't need to** stop for petrol.

✗ They **needn't have** stopped for petrol.

	The person did the action	It was not necessary
needn't have	Yes	True
didn't need to	We don't know.	True

You needn't have made a cake. (= You DID make a cake. It was not necessary.)

You didn't need to make a cake. (= You DID make a cake. It was not necessary.
OR
You DIDN'T make a cake. It was not necessary.)

Two different possible meanings!

We often use *needn't have* and *didn't need to* with *worry / worried*.
I thought they'd all be late, but I needn't have worried. Everyone came on time.
You didn't need to worry about me. I finished the race without any problems.

1 Are *needn't have* and *didn't need to* both possible? Tick
(✓) if both are possible. Cross out *needn't have* if it is not
possible.

a Thank you for your lovely present. You *didn't need to
buy / needn't have bought* one for us. ✓

b It's good that you didn't come to work this morning.
You *didn't need to be / needn't have been* at the
8 o'clock meeting. ....

c She gave her hairdresser a £10 tip! Why? She *didn't
need to do that / needn't have done that.* ....

d Olga took the train to Moscow. She *didn't need to fly /
needn't have flown.* ....

e I got home at 2 a.m. My parents waited up until I came
back! They *didn't need to do that / needn't have done
that!* ....

f Why did you stop our football game? You *didn't need
to stop / needn't have stopped* it so early! ....

2 Make *needn't have* sentences to say to Bill.

a Bill ran to the bus stop. The bus never came!
You needn't have run to the bus stop.

b Bill worried about Judy. There were no problems and she
was fine!

....

c Bill remembered that he had £5,000 in a savings account
after he borrowed £2,000 from the bank.

....

d Bill queued for ten hours to buy a concert ticket. Then a
friend offered him one for free.

....

e A Science exam was cancelled after Bill studied all night for it!

....

f Bill took his laptop to work, but didn't use it all day.

....

3 Which picture is best for each sentence?

a 1 .... 2 ....

Oh, Timmy! You needn't have brought a
pizza. We've already got a huge one.

b 1 .... 2 ....

Thank you, Jenny! You needn't have got
me a present.

c 1 .... 2 ....

You needn't have washed the car, Pete.
The garage is going to do it later today.

More practice

can (ability, possibility, request), **could** (request, past ability), **should**

ability or possibility	can/can't	I **can** play baseball. We **can't** finish our homework. **Can** you use a webcam with it?
permission	can/can't	You **can** work at Jenny's desk. I **can't** borrow Mum's car without her permission. **Can** I come in?
	could	You **could** take lunch early today if you want. **Could** I make a suggestion?
ability in the past	could/couldn't	Noel **could** understand everything Chrissie said. Joe **couldn't** find the lost money. **Could** you play piano well when you were young?
ask for help	can/could	**Can** you carry my bags, please? **Could** you lend me $10?
tell people what to do or give advice	should/shouldn't	You **should** do it again. Robert **shouldn't** tell Jake about the boat. **Should** I take the exam?

1 Complete the sentences with *can, can't, could* or *couldn't*. (Different answers are possible.)

a My little sister is amazing. She ___can___ do three fantastic magic tricks.

b Excuse me! _____ you help me? I'm lost.

c When I lived in Paris I _____ speak French so I talked with my hands instead!

d Freddie is very puzzled! He _____ understand why you aren't talking to him.

e My dad was terrible in the kitchen. He didn't know how to make toast and he _____ boil an egg!

f Sorry! That room is private. You _____ go in there.

g Petra walked up and down the hotel corridor. Which was her door? She _____ remember the room number!

h Oh dear! I feel very hot. _____ you get me a cold drink, please?

2 Give advice or orders with *should*. (Different answers are possible.)

a Your fifteen-year-old child doesn't want to do her homework, but you think it is important.

You should do your homework.

b Your eight-year-old cousin says she feels tired. It's very late!

c Your friend is feeling very ill. She says, 'I don't want to go to the doctor.'

d Your friend doesn't know many English words. She will fail her vocabulary test next week.

e Your friend wants to eat the last piece of pizza. But her mum hasn't had any yet!

3 Match the sentences with the meanings.

a Can we come in?
b David couldn't sing very well when he was a teenager.
c You should take some aspirin and go to bed.
d Could someone help me carry this cupboard, please?
e Sheila can use my phone if she is very careful with it!
f We can't use the PC! It's broken.

1 ability in the past
2 asking for help
3 asking for permission
4 talking about possibility
5 telling people what to do or giving advice
6 giving permission

4 *INTERNET* QUIZ 🔍

Complete the quotations by famous people. Use the phrases in the box. Use the internet if you need help.

> and you're halfway there   but everyone can help someone
> if I could do all I can?   it can only become stairs
> it's day-to-day living that wears you out
> we must first believe that we can   you're right

a Theodore Roosevelt (26th President of the USA): 'Believe you can *and you're halfway there* _____'.

b Henry Ford (industrialist, developer of automated building of motor cars): 'If you think you can do a thing or think you can't do a thing, _____'.

c Nikos Kazantzakis (author of *Zorba the Greek*): 'In order to succeed, _____'.

d Ronald Reagan (film actor, 40th President of the USA): 'We can't help everyone, _____'.

e Anton Chekhov (Russian author of *The Cherry Orchard*): 'Any idiot can face a crisis; _____'.

f Sun Tzu (Chinese general, author of *The Art of War*: 'Can you imagine what I would do _____'.

g Mitch Heidberg (American stand-up comedian): 'An escalator can never break; _____'.

I can ... Talk about past and future abilities

be able to (past and future)

Now I **can** play the violin and three other instruments.

By the time I'm 30 I'**ll be able to** play lots more.

I **could** play the piano when I was just four years old.

Then I tried to learn the guitar. I **couldn't** play it very well! But I **was able to** learn a few tunes.

But I'm sure ... I still **won't be able to** play the guitar very well.

Past		Present		Future	
You/We/They	were able to	I	am able to		
I/He/She/It	was able to	You/We/They	are able to	I/You/He/She/It/We/They	'll be able to / will be able to
		He/She/It	is able to		
I/You/He/She/It/We/They	could	I/You/He/She/It/We/They	can		

We mostly use *could* for things you were <u>generally</u> able to do in the past, but NOT for things you did just once.

We mostly use *was / were able to* for things that you did **on one occasion** in the past.

✓ I could use an iPad when I was two years old! ← general ability

✗ ~~I could repair your broken plate.~~

✓ I was able to repair your broken plate.

at **one** time or in **one** situation

We make past negatives with either *wasn't / weren't able to* or *couldn't*. There is no difference in meaning or use.

✓ I couldn't finish my homework.

✓ I wasn't able to finish my homework.

✓ The team weren't able to score any goals in the second half.

We make future negatives with *won't be able to* (= will not be able to).

I'm sorry, but I won't be able to come to your lecture.

1 You worked on your company's new products team last month. Say what you *were able* to do and what you *couldn't* do.

a (design two new models ✓)

We were able to design two new models.

b (make a larger size ✗)

We couldn't make a larger size.

c (solve a problem with the antenna ✓)

d (go to a conference in Dubai ✓)

e (meet lots of programmers from around the world ✓)

f (find a way to make it more economically ✗)

g (improve the software ✓)

2 Is *could* possible? If it is not possible in a sentence, cross out *could* and rewrite the sentence with *was/were able*.

a I could play the piano when I was three.

✓

b I could finish the Fire Safety report last Friday.

✗ *I was able to finish the Fire Safety report last Friday.*

c I could cook a great meal for Benny when he came round yesterday.

d I could run quite fast until I broke my leg last year.

e I could watch the video when I was on my lunch break.

f When I was a teenager I could beat anybody at online racing games.

3 Complete the sentences with *can, am/is/are able to, could, was/were able to* or *'ll be able to*. (In some questions different answers are possible.)

a I was always interested in design. When I was young, I __could / was able to__ make beautiful jewellery presents for my family and friends.

b I studied Fine Art at university and .... take part in a student exhibition in my final year.

c Some well-known jewellers .... see my work at that exhibition, and I was offered a job at Tollabby's.

d So, nowadays I .... work with wonderful materials – gold, platinum, diamonds and other gemstones.

e I'm very lucky. Next year, I .... to go to India for nine months and study traditional designs.

4 *ABOUT* YOU

Make some sentences about things you could/ couldn't do (or will/won't be able to do) at different ages. You can use ideas from the boxes or your own ideas. (Many different answers are possible.)

> 5   10   15   20   ~~60~~   75   ~~at university~~
> in my first job   in Primary School

> ~~cook supper~~   drive a car   make a Lego house
> play the guitar   speak German

a *When I was 16 I could ride a motorbike.*

b *When I was at university I couldn't cook my own supper.*

c *When I'm 60 I'll be able to relax!*

d ....

e ....

f ....

g ....

I can ... Talk about things which were possible, but didn't happen

could(n't) have

Thank you. You're very kind. You know ... I **could have been** a big pop star.

I **could've won!**

What a terrible picnic! We missed the train. I lost the map. It's rained all day.

It **could've been** worse. We still have the food!

Did they tell you that this is a fancy dress party?

Yes! Of course!

Well ... they **could have told** me!

Thanks for my bedtime story, Mum. It was lovely but ...it **could have been** a bit more exciting! And it **could have had** more monsters.

Goodnight, darling!

You **could have cooked** a little more.

We use **could have** (or *could've*) + past participle to talk about things that were possible, but which did NOT happen. We sometimes use *could have* to criticise someone.

You could have told me. = You didn't tell me AND I wish that you had told me.

You could have cooked more. = You didn't cook a lot of food AND I wish that you had cooked more.

People often say *It could have been worse!* This means: the situation is bad, but I can imagine something even worse (that didn't happen) ... so we shouldn't be too unhappy!

You use the negative *couldn't have* to say that something was not possible to do.

I didn't finish the essay – but we only had two days. I couldn't have finished it in that short time.

I didn't want to go to that meal last night, but I couldn't have refused.

We can use *couldn't have* to sympathise or to comfort people who have done something which they regret.

A: *It was awful! I asked him about his job. He said he was sacked two weeks ago!*
B: *You couldn't have known.*

A: *I really wanted to help my grandma.*
B: *You couldn't have done more.*

1 You are upset because some people didn't do some important things. What do you say to them? Start with 'Oh …' and the person's name.

a Jeremy didn't tell you about his car problem.

You say: _Oh, Jeremy! You could've told me about your car problem!_

b Susie didn't write a blog entry about your photos.

You say: _Oh, Susie! You could've written a blog entry about my photos!_

c Sandra didn't ask for help.

You say: ....

d Mary didn't come on time.

You say: ....

e Tommy didn't buy any cakes for the party.

You say: ....

f Jo didn't leave her dog at home.

You say: ....

g Jenny didn't make her bed.

You say: ....

2 Write one or more comments with *could have* to criticise yourself or suggest alternative possibilities you didn't take. (Many different answers are possible.)

a You have just walked up eight floors to talk to your friend, Olga. You are exhausted!

I could have used the lift!

I could have walked more slowly.

I could have phoned her.

b You have walked across town in the rain. You are tired and wet!

....

....

c You failed an English grammar test.

....

....

....

d You stayed at a party until 3 a.m. last night. It's the next day now and you are at work, feeling terrible!

....

....

e You bought an expensive new car – but you have very little money.

....

....

f You have put up some wallpaper very badly because you didn't know how to do it properly.

....

....

....

3 Complete Barbara's replies to Ian. In each sentence, use *couldn't have* and a verb from the box.

afford̶ explain go imagine know

a Ian: I wanted to borrow $3,000 from my bank – but they refused!

Barbara: I'm glad! ... You _couldn't have afforded_ to pay it back.

b Ian: I really wanted to see that concert!

Barbara: We .... ! We didn't have tickets.

c Ian: I asked Andrew about his girlfriend Susan, and he started crying!

Barbara: They split up a few days ago! But you .... that.

d Ian: I told the doctor how to get to the exhibition hall and he still got lost!

Barbara: It's his fault! You .... more clearly.

e Ian: I've made the cake.

Barbara: Wow! It's beautiful! I .... that it would be so lovely.

I can ... Tell the story of an adventure

Verb + **to** infinitive

W Walk the world

Home > Blog > **Walking diary**

When I was 14, I decided to walk around the world. I wanted to be the youngest person ever to do that. I hoped to finish the walk in less than seven years. I planned to start in America. My parents agreed to give me $3,000 dollars to pay for equipment and some large companies also offered to help. Anyway, on my 16th birthday I started to walk westwards from New York. I began to feel tired very soon, but after a few weeks I learned to enjoy it. I had lots of problems. Once I tried to go too fast and I needed to rest my legs for three days. One evening, I accidentally stepped on a long green snake. It raised its head and threatened to bite me. I ran on quickly! But I continued to make good progress every day. I promised to call my parents every day – but I often forgot to phone them! I'm now in Los Angeles! I failed to get on a boat to Australia last week because the captain refused to let me on board– but I've arranged to catch a cargo ship to Australia next week! I expect to enjoy a nice long rest!

All these verbs go with the *to* infinitive

agree	to give	expect	to enjoy	need	to rest	start	to walk
arrange	to catch	fail	to get on	offer	to help	threaten	to bite
begin	to feel	forget	to take	plan	to start	try	to go
continue	to make	hope	to finish	promise	to phone	want	to be
decide	to walk	learn	to enjoy	refuse	to allow		

For most of these verbs, it's wrong to use them with *-ing*.

✓ *I decided to walk.*

✗ *I decided walking.*

✓ *I forgot to phone my parents.*

✗ *I forgot phoning my parents.*

Some verbs can be used with the *to* infinitive or *-ing*. The meaning is the same.

I started to walk. = **I started walking.**

I began to walk. = **I began walking.**

I continued to walk. = **I continued walking.**

1 Complete the sentences using the correct form of the two verbs in brackets. Decide which verb comes first!

a Thomas _decided to take_ a break and have a coffee. (take / decide)

b Eloise _____ her parents about the charity collection at school. (tell / forget)

c The shop assistant _____ the angry customer his money back. (agree / give)

d Please sit down! I _____ my reasons to you. (explain / need)

e Thank goodness! George has _____ me his bicycle. (lend / offer)

f Will you be in town next week? I _____ you at the meeting. (see / hope)

g Alice _____ when she was only 16. (drive / learn)

h I wasn't able to check that report myself. Luckily, Adam _____ . (agree / help)

i The guard _____ us out if we made any more noise. (throw / threaten)

2 Complete the story using pairs of verbs from the box.

> begin / discuss   decide / fly   expect / stay
> forget / do   hope / see   refuse / allow
> start / look for   try / travel   ~~want / have~~

When we left college, my best friend Ellie and I both _wanted to have_ ᵃ a big adventure before we _____ ᵇ a serious job. We _____ ᶜ all the things we could do and finally _____ ᵈ to Kenya and _____ ᵉ around the country using just buses and trains. We _____ ᶠ lots of wildlife.
When we were on the plane, Ellie said 'I think we _____ ᵍ one important thing. We didn't get visas.' I was so upset. I thought that the border officials would _____ ʰ us in. But, luckily, it wasn't a problem. We were able to buy visas at the airport – and we had a great time. We _____ ⁱ for two months. That didn't happen! I came home after two weeks, but Ellie met a handsome Kenyan and married him. She still lives there. That was a big adventure!

3 Make some short stories using the three verbs in the same order as in the question. (Many different answers are possible.)

a decide   start   offer

Ralph decided to go into town. He started to walk.
Then his friend Dominic drove past and offered to
give him a lift.

b want   forget   try

_____
_____
_____

c arrange   refuse   promise

_____
_____
_____

d fail   refuse   threaten

_____
_____
_____
_____

e begin   decide   hope

_____
_____
_____

Talk about things I like and dislike doing

Verb + -ing

Hi, Greta. It's me. Do you **feel like going out** tonight?

I'm bored ... and I **can't stand watching** another soap opera on TV.

Oh ... you need to **finish studying**. OK. Speak to you later!

Hi, Shari. Yes, Tom here! Do you **fancy having** some Indian food tonight?

Oh. You've **given up eating** carbohydrates this month! And you want to **avoid eating** any spicy food. OK. Another time then! See you. Bye.

Oh dear, I really **hate going** to restaurants on my own.

Hello? Oh hi, Marcella. What a nice surprise.

No, of course I **don't mind helping** you with that problem. Can I **suggest having** an Indian meal after we've finished?

Or ... do you **fancy trying** that new Thai restaurant? Actually, I always have Indian food, so I'm quite **keen on having** something different.

Yes, I really **love trying** new cuisines. I always **enjoy tasting** new dishes.

It's delicious. I can't **imagine cooking** this at home!

Oh ... I **like making** unusual dishes. I **love experimenting** with new ingredients. But there's nobody to try them ...

OK. 8.30. Great. I'm really **looking forward to seeing** you again.

Well ...

admit	
avoid	
can't stand	
dislike	
enjoy	
fancy	
feel like	
finish	
give up	*-ing*
hate	
imagine	
like	
look forward to	
love	
mind*	
miss	
prefer	
suggest	

✗ *I finished to write my essay.*
✓ *I finished writing my essay.*
✗ *I enjoy to eat fresh fish.*
✓ *I enjoy eating fresh fish.*

Don't forget that negatives also take -ing.
I don't feel like going out tonight.
I can't imagine working for that awful boss!
I don't like seeing people cry.
I don't mind locking up after the meeting.

Some of these verbs can also be followed by *to* infinitive with the same meaning:

hate	*I hate to make spelling mistakes.*
	I hate making spelling mistakes.
like / don't like	*I don't like to read the news.*
	I don't like reading the news.
love	*I love to watch a good film.*
	I love watching a good film.
prefer	*I prefer to study alone.*
	I prefer studying alone.

mind is usually used in questions and negative sentences

1 Complete the sentences using the verbs in brackets in the correct form.

a Tina dislikes ____going____ to the dentist. (go)

b Harry really enjoys _____ the saxophone. (play)

c We're all looking forward to _____ you on Sunday. (see)

d I can't stand _____ that programme. (watch)

e Has Sandra finished _____ her homework yet? (do)

f I avoid _____ anything about a film before I see it. (read)

g Has Mabel finally given up _____ ? (smoke)

h Now that my children are at university, I miss _____ them around the house. (have)

i The teacher cleverly avoided _____ them the answer. (tell)

j We all imagined _____ the top prize. (win)

k The boys felt like _____ some ice creams. (get)

l Orlando didn't mind _____ the show. (miss)

m The class suggested _____ the task again another day. (try)

2 Use the two verbs in the correct form to complete the sentences. You may need to change their order.

a We were in Australia last winter and really ____enjoyed swimming____ in the warm sea. (swim / enjoy)

b The decorators had a long coffee break, then went back into the room and _____ the walls. (paint / finish)

c When Mrs Trevis was 60, she _____ _____ and started work as a counsellor. (give up / teach)

d Our department manager _____ _____ at 3 p.m. to discuss the crisis. (meet / suggest)

e Gerry has never met his Australian cousins. He _____ _____ them next week. (look forward to / see)

f After the police stopped him, the coach driver _____ _____ at 150 kph on the motorway. (drive / admit)

g Although I dislike most dairy products, I _____ _____ a little cheese sometimes. (don't mind / eat)

h I've bought some cakes for the party although usually I _____ _____ my own. (make / prefer)

remember, stop + to infinitive / **-ing**

> Please switch off the lights when you leave.

> Time to go home. What did she ask me to do? Ah, yes … switch off the lights.

He **remembered to** do it!

> Good! I **remembered to switch** off the lights.

> Oh dear. I can't remember. Did I switch off the lights?

> Yes. I **remember switching** off the lights!

He **remembered doing** it!

Remember can be used with the *to* infinitive or *-ing* … BUT they have a different meaning.
You *remember to do something* BEFORE you do it. (i.e. you think about what you need to do)
You *remember doing something* AFTER you do it. (i.e. you think about what you have already done)

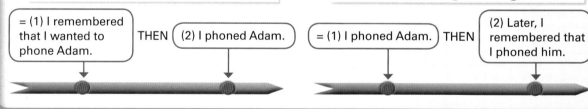

I **remembered to phone** Adam.

= (1) I remembered that I wanted to phone Adam.   THEN   (2) I phoned Adam.

I **remembered phoning** Adam.

= (1) I phoned Adam.   THEN   (2) Later, I remembered that I phoned him.

Stop is similar to *remember*. It can be used with the *to infinitive* or *-ing*
…with a different meaning.

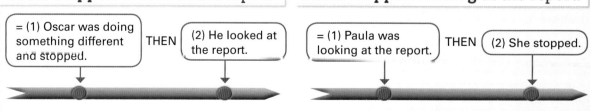

Oscar **stopped to look** at the report.

= (1) Oscar was doing something different and stopped.   THEN   (2) He looked at the report.

Paula **stopped looking** at the report.

= (1) Paula was looking at the report.   THEN   (2) She stopped.

1 Read the story and the sentences. Put a tick (✓) if each sentence is true according to the story. If it isn't true, put a cross (✗).

'I'm going to visit Grandma,' said Alex. His mum smiled. 'Tell her about our new cat and invite her to come round for lunch on Sunday,' she said. 'Oh – and could you go to the shop on your way home and get some milk and 12 eggs?' 'Sure,' said Alex.

His sister phoned him. 'I left home a few minutes ago, but I forgot to feed the cat,' she said. 'Could you do it, please?' Alex went to look for a tin of cat food in the kitchen cupboard. His dad came up and started chatting to him about football.

After about ten minutes Alex said, 'Sorry, Dad. I really have to go!' He finally left the house – then suddenly thought, 'Oh, no! After all that, I forgot the cat!' He ran back inside, fed the cat and then went out to catch the bus to his grandma's flat. Unfortunately,

he didn't have his monthly ticket with him, so he had to pay the fare.

Alex told his gran about the new cat. She showed him some photos of when he was very young. 'Did I really go to Paris?' 'Yes – but you were very small! And look at this photo of you flying a kite.' 'Ah – yes … I remember that day!' said Alex.

He walked home at about 5.00 and bought some milk on the way.

When he got home, his mum asked him, 'Did you tell Grandma about the cat?' 'Um … yes – she's looking forward to seeing it,' said Alex. 'Did you do the shopping?' 'Um … let me think … yes, I definitely went to the shop!'

a Alex's sister remembered to feed the cat before she left the house.   ✗

b Alex stopped to talk to his dad before he left the house.   ✓

c Alex stopped talking to his dad after about 10 minutes.   ....

d Alex remembered to feed the cat before he caught the bus.   ....

e Alex remembered to take his bus ticket with him.   ....

f Alex remembered to tell his grandma about the cat.   ....

g Alex remembered to tell her about the lunch invitation.   ....

h Alex remembered going to Paris when he was very young.   ....

i Alex remembered flying a kite when he was small.   ....

j Alex remembered to go to the shop.   ....

k Alex remembered to buy some milk on his way home.   ....

l Alex remembered to buy some eggs on his way home.   ....

m Alex remembered telling his grandma about the cat.   ....

n Alex remembered going to the shop.   ....

2 ABOUT YOU

Answer the questions.

a Write down four things you remember doing when you were ten years old or younger.

1 *I remember telling my teacher that her lesson was very boring!*

2 ....

3 ....

4 ....

b Write down four things that you must remember to do in the next week.

1 *I must remember to go online and book seats for the concert.*

2 ....

3 ....

4 ....

c Write down something that you have stopped doing this year.

1 *I've stopped going to the gym every day.*

2 ....

More practice

Use *forget, try* and *manage to*

forget + *to* infinitive, **never forget** + *-ing*, **try** + *to* infinitive, **try** + *-ing*, **manage to** + infinitive

Agh! This stupid computer doesn't start up.

Try holding Function key 1 when you switch it on.

Could you try to finish that presentation by lunchtime, please?

Well ... I'll try to do it.

Jacob says he'll never forget losing that Brazilian order!

Oh no! I forgot to order more printer ink!

I tried asking the boss about an extra holiday. No luck!

Hurray! I managed to win a 20,000 unit order for Poland.

Have you managed to contact the Japanese office yet?

Not yet! I'll try calling them now.

Forget **is usually used with *to* infinitive.**

✗ *Oh no! I forgot ~~giving her~~ the present!*

✓ *Oh no! I forgot to give her the present!*

After *will never forget* we use verb +-*ing*.

✓ *I'll never forget meeting the boys in my favourite band.*

Try **is possible with both *to infinitive* and *-ing*. There is a small difference in meaning.**

You *try doing something* when you are experimenting and want to see what happens. Often, you hope that you will find a good result or an answer to your problems.

We tried making pancakes with different ingredients.

Christina tried changing the oil, replacing the batteries and polishing the machinery, but it still didn't work!

You *try to do something* when it is difficult to do and you are not certain if it is possible. Maybe you can't actually finish the thing you want to do.

Masumi tried to open the classroom window, but it was completely stuck.

He tried to finish the homework, but gave up after an hour.

Manage to + infinitive

When you *manage to do something*:
→ you try
→ it is difficult
→ but you succeed!

Alison managed to win the marathon. = **She tried to win the marathon + It was difficult + She won the marathon!**

I managed to finish the report before midnight. = **I tried to finish the report before midnight + It was difficult + I finished it before midnight!**

 The verb *manage to* is completely different from the verb *manage* (which means organise and control).

Manage to has no connection with business management!

The verb *manage to*:
He managed to climb the mountain.

The verb *manage*:
He managed the Sales department very well.

1 Complete the sentences using the verbs in brackets in the correct form. (Different answers may be possible.)

a The bus driver tried ___to close___ the doors while we were still getting on. (close)

b The development team managed _____ a stronger screen for the product. (make)

c Your leg is healing very quickly after the accident. Try _____ across the room. (walk)

d I forgot _____ that DVD you asked for. (get)

e I'll never forget _____ that film with you on our first date! (watch)

f You won't forget _____ me again tonight, will you? (call)

g My boss wouldn't want to try _____ on my low salary! (live)

h Have you managed _____ the oven yet? (mend)

i My car's making strange noises. I've tried _____ the oil, but it doesn't make any difference. (change)

2 ABOUT YOU

Answer the questions.

a Write down four things you forgot to do in the last month.

1 *I forgot to send off my exam entry.*

2 _____

3 _____

4 _____

b Write down three things that you will try to do in the next week.

1 *I'll try to go to bed earlier.*

2 _____

3 _____

4 _____

c Write down something that you managed to do recently.

1 *I managed to get 73 marks in my History test.*

2 _____

I can ...

Describe conversations with other people

Verb + preposition collocations

So ... last night ...

I called Millie's house – but her dad answered ... so I **talked to** her dad first and he **asked about** our project, so I **explained** the work **to** him.

Then I **asked for** Millie and I **chatted with** her for ages! Oh, we **talked about** everything! We **chatted about** music and TV and film stars and boys.

Then we **argued about** something and she **shouted at** me and I **swore at** her. Then I **apologised to** her and she **apologised for** her rudeness.

Then we **gossiped about** our classmates and **complained about** our exams and she **told** me **about** Tommy and I **laughed at** her silly story and ...

oh ... we **talked for** more than two hours ...

talk / speak / chat	to*	someone	(about something)
	with*		
	for	(time)	
	about	something	

* *Talk with* and *speak with* are more common in the USA. *Talk to* and *speak to* are more common in the UK.

listen	to	something / someone

| argue / gossip | with | someone | (about something) |
| | about | something | (with someone) |

apologise / complain	to	someone	(about something)
	about	something	
apologise	for	something	

| shout / swear | at | someone | (about something) |

ask	someone	(about something)
	about	someone
	for	someone

You want some information about this person.

You want to speak to this person.

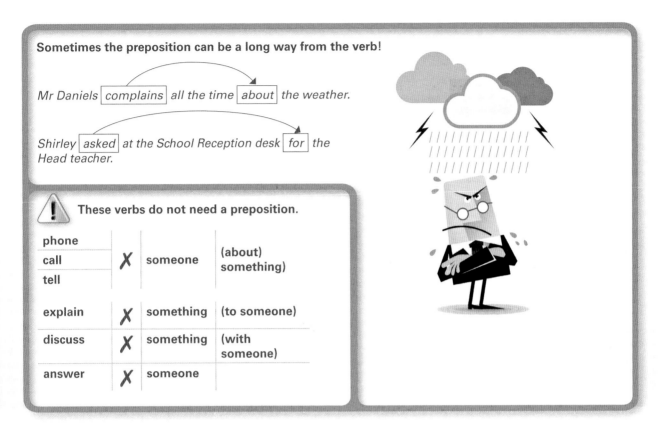

Sometimes the preposition can be a long way from the verb!

Mr Daniels complains all the time about the weather.

Shirley asked at the School Reception desk for the Head teacher.

⚠ **These verbs do not need a preposition.**

phone			
call	✗	someone	(about) something)
tell			
explain	✗	something	(to someone)
discuss	✗	something	(with someone)
answer	✗	someone	

1 Underline the correct word. Ø means no preposition.

a We were chatting all evening *of* / *about* her performance.

b The children apologised *to* / *at* the teacher for their bad behaviour.

c Jerzy listened carefully *to* / *at* the lecturer, but thought she was very boring.

d It was a great meeting! We discussed *about* / *Ø* the new Canadian products.

e The builders argued *on* / *about* the best materials to use.

f Sue and Judy chatted on their mobiles *for* / *with* two or three hours!

g We were talking *on* / *about* our favourite fast food!

h That horrid guard just swore *to* / *at* me!

i I gossiped *with* / *to* my friends all evening

j We gossiped *on* / *about* Cheryl and Ken all evening.

k The pilots talked *with* / *for* / *Ø* the airport supervisors, but couldn't agree what to do.

l The pilots phoned *with* / *to* / *Ø* the airport supervisors, but couldn't agree what to do.

m The pilots and the airport supervisors talked *with* / *for* / *at* twenty minutes, but couldn't agree what to do.

n When Ted asked *with* / *to* / *Ø* Julie to marry him, she answered *with* / *to* / *Ø* him very quickly.

2 Fill in the missing prepositions in this phone conversation. If there is no preposition, write Ø.

Caller: Hello. Could I speak __to__ ᵃ Mr Reynolds, please?

Receptionist: Who's calling __Ø__ ᵇ him?

Caller: My name is Jeff King. I need to discuss _____ᶜ a problem with him.

Receptionist: I'm sorry. I've forgotten. Do you want to talk _____ᵈ Mrs Holbein?

Caller: No! I asked _____ᵉ Mr Reynolds.

Receptionist: I'm sorry, sir. Mr Reynolds is out. Would you like to explain your problem _____ᶠ Mrs Holbein?

Caller: No, thank you. I have to speak to him _____ᵍ something confidential. When he gets in, please tell _____ʰ him that Jeff King called. Say that I want to ask him _____ⁱ the Rotterdam contract.

get = receive

Did you get my letter?

Henry got $50 from his parents.

I got 87% in the English exam.

Kelly asked him three times, but she didn't get an answer.

The team finally got permission to climb the mountain.

get = buy / pay for

Can I get a latte, please?

I went into town and got a new book.

Nora got her new carpet for just £5!

What are you getting for her birthday?

'Oh, here's the lunch bill.' 'Put your purse away! I'll get it!'

get = become

We're getting married next year.

Let's go inside. I'm getting cold.

Terry got really angry with his friends.

The girls wanted to come to the race, but they both got ill last night.

Your grandparents are getting old.

get = answer the door or phone

Was that the doorbell? I'll get it.

Could someone get the phone, please? I'm busy.

get = arrive somewhere

The train got here very late.

They finally got to the station.

We're going to get to Doha after midnight.

When will you get home?

It takes about three hours to get there.

get to home, get to there ✗

get = take a vehicle

I'm getting a plane to Rio.

Mike's going to get the 7.25 train.

Will Sheila get a taxi from the airport?

I don't want to walk. I think I'll get the bus.

get = make / prepare a meal

I'll get breakfast!

Who's going to get supper?

get = fetch*

Could you get me a towel, please?

I'm just going to get my glasses so I can read this.

You look cold. I'll go upstairs and get you a jumper.

***fetch** = go and find something and bring it back*

---

1 What is the meaning of *got* in each sentence? Match the sentences with the correct meanings.

> arrived somewhere   became   bought/paid for
> received   took a vehicle

a I got my certificate from the examiners.
Meaning = *received*

b Sheila got really hungry during the athletics event.
Meaning = ...

c We got to the airport at midnight.
Meaning = ...

d Charlie finally got an answer from the university.
Meaning = ...

e The children got really noisy after lunch!
Meaning = ...

f I didn't need a lift. I got the bus.
Meaning = ...

g The Saunders got home before their daughter.
Meaning = ...

h I got all the shopping at the corner shop.
Meaning = ...

i When did they get to the conference centre?
Meaning = ...

2 Rewrite each sentence using *get*.

a Susan arrived at the meeting twenty minutes late.
Susan got to the meeting twenty minutes late.

b Marisa said she'll make lunch for everyone.
....

c I hope we can catch the 10.25 train or we'll be late.
....

d Sorry. I can't answer the phone because my hands are dirty.
....

e Do you know what you're receiving for your birthday?
....

f I quite like Andrew, but I'm becoming very annoyed at his rude comments.
....

g Helen bought some fantastic new shoes in town today.
....

I can ...

Tell the story of how I met a new friend

Multi-word verbs

My girlfriend **broke up** with me.

She **dropped** me **off** at home then said goodbye ... forever!

I tried to phone her. After three days, I **gave up**.

I needed to **get away**! Somewhere interesting.

Three days later, my plane **took off** for Italy!

I **checked into** an amazing hotel. While I was **filling in** some forms, I noticed a really cool girl.

We **bumped into** each other three times the next day.

I **asked** her **out**! After that, we **went out** every night.

Then I **found out** that she already had a boyfriend!

I **checked out** of the hotel.

Hey! Don't **walk out on** me! That was my brother!

We're **getting on** really well now. I finally **got over** my ex!

(**Main verb**) + (**particle** (i.e. a preposition or adverb)) = a **multi-word verb**

He's really | looking | forward | *to the holidays.*

(He's waiting for them with excitement and happiness.)

Pauline | looks | after | *her disabled mother.*

(She cares for her, gives her food, helps her, etc.)

I often | look | up | *new words in my electronic dictionary.*

(I search for and find information about them.)

⚠️ Not all combinations of a verb and a preposition or adverb are multi-word verbs.

For example, *I looked through the window* is just the normal main verb *looked* and a preposition that tells you the direction of the action.

It is often impossible to guess the meaning of multi-word verbs. You can't guess the meaning of *went off* by thinking about the meanings of *went* and *off*. In fact *go off* has many possible meanings (depending on the situation) e.g.

The bomb went off. (= it exploded)

The cheese went off. (= it got old and became bad. Perhaps I left it in the fridge for too long!)

The electricity went off. (= it suddenly stopped working.)

You need to learn the grammar of each multi-word verb.

Some multi-word verbs do not need an object:
The plane took off.

Other multi-word verbs take an object:
We checked into the hotel.

Sometimes we can split up the words of a multi-word verb.
I've already filled the form in.

And this is also good:
I've already filled in the form.

Pronouns must come before the particle.
✓ *I've filled it in.*   ✗ *I've filled in it.*

Some multi-word verbs can never be separated.
✓ *I bumped into Susan.* ✓ *I bumped into her.*
✗ *I bumped Susan into.* ✗ *I bumped her into.*

1 Here are some ideas from the story on page 168 – but all the multi-word verbs have been changed! Can you put the multi-word verbs back – without looking back at the original story?

a My girlfriend ended the relationship with me.

My girlfriend broke up with me.

b I needed to escape.

c My plane started flying.

d I registered at an amazing hotel.

e I wrote information on some forms.

f We met each other by accident.

g I invited her for a date.

h We had a date every night.

i I discovered that she already had a boyfriend.

j I left the hotel.

2 Complete the sentences with *off, on, out, into, from, with* or *of*.

a I've known Sylvie for years. We get ___on___ really well together.

b After his plane took _____ , Rob fell asleep and didn't wake up till it landed!

c Michelle started a course on karate, but she gave _____ after a few weeks.

d I thinks she's really beautiful, but I'm too shy to ask her _____ .

e 'Thanks very much for the lift! Could you drop me _____ at the station?'

f Sandra bumped _____ Aggie at the market this morning. They hadn't met for years.

g Eddy hated the Luxus Hotel. After just two hours there, he checked _____ and moved across the road to a better one.

h Before you can start using the online forum, you have to fill _____ your personal details on a form.

I can ...

Say that I feel the same as someone else

so do I, neither do I

I enjoyed that exhibition.

So did I.

I don't like the crowds.

Neither do I.

I'm definitely coming back next year!

So am I.

I've never been to Venice before.

Neither have I.

I love this bridge!

So do I.

I think this is so romantic!

So do I.

Tom doesn't want to go home and neither do I.

My sister was at last year's carnival!

So was I.

Use *so do I* to say that you feel the same (or do the same) as someone else's positive statement.

Use *neither do I* to say that you feel the same (or do the same) as someone's negative statement.

| I love | old buildings.

So do I.

Present Simple

| I don't like | old buildings.

Neither do I.

Present Simple

= I also do not like old buildings.

| I walk | to work.

So do I.

| I don't play | tennis.

Neither do I.

Use *so am I* / *neither am I* for Present Progressive sentences.

| I'm leaving | at midnight. | So am I.
| I'm not having | any dessert. | Neither am I.

Use *so was I* / *neither was I* for Past Simple *be*.

| I was | very cold. | So was I.
| I wasn't | ready. | Neither was I.

Use *so did I* / *neither did I* for other Past Simple sentences.

| I bought | a T-shirt. | So did I.
| I didn't buy | a keyring. | Neither did I.

Use *so have I* / *neither have I* for Present Perfect sentences.

| I've been | to Rome. | So have I.
| I haven't seen | the answers. | Neither have I.

1 Mark feels the same way as Annie or does similar things. Match her comments and his responses.

Annie's comments
a I was really bored in that lesson!
b I usually enjoy Chemistry lessons.
c … but I'm not enjoying this week's Economics questions.
d I've done the Physics homework.
e I haven't finished them yet.
f I don't want to ask for help.
g I looked for information on the internet yesterday.
h Anyway, I'm going home now.

Mark's responses
1 So do I.
2 Neither do I.
3 So was I.
4 So am I.
5 So did I.
6 Neither have I.
7 So have I.
8 Neither am I.

2 Read these statements, then reply to say that you feel (or do) the same.
a I like strawberry milkshakes!   So do I.
b I was really angry.
c I loved the film.
d I hated the film.
e I didn't like the film.
f I've been to London before.
g I'm not waiting here!
h I don't want to go.

Understand young people's colloquial conversations

was like in direct speech and other colloquial UK English grammar

You know, I saw Reece yesterday.

> You know

And he **was like**, 'Hi!'

> was like

And I **was like**, 'Hi!'

> was like

And he **goes**, 'You coming to the party?'

> goes   Word missed out

And I **was like**, 'Whatever!'

> was like   Whatever

And he **goes**, 'Hayden's band's **gonna** play.'

> gonna

And I was like 'Oh, I **so** love that band!'

> so

So he goes, 'OK. You **wanna** come, then?'

> Word missed out   wanna

And I was like, 'I'm **so** gonna be there!

> so

 There are many different kinds of English. People speak different English in different countries. And even inside the same country, people speak and write in many different ways.

The English in this book is based on standard 'educated' English as people use it in UK schools, colleges, businesses, on radio, TV, etc. and in many other formal and informal situations.

This unit is different! Be careful! The language on this page would be marked wrong in most English language exams! However, this is slang – everyday informal English – and it's how many young people speak in the United Kingdom. Even if you don't want to speak like this yourself, it's useful to know about these features so that you can understand people you meet or when you watch films.

you know	*You know* is often used to start a new topic. It suggests that the subject will be something the other person is familiar with or interested in.
was like goes	*was like* or *goes* are alternatives to *he/she said* or *he/she asked.* They introduce a piece of direct speech i.e. the actual words the person spoke. *She said, 'Hi!' = She was like, 'Hi'* *He said, 'Nice trainers!' = 'He goes, 'Nice trainers!'*
words missed out	Words are often missed out and sentences are shortened. In this conversation, the auxiliary verbs *are* and *do* have been missed out of two questions. *'You coming to the party?'* ➜ *'Are you coming to the party?'* *'You wanna come?'* ➜ *'Do you want to come?'*
whatever	*Whatever* means 'yes if you like', but it can mean 'I'm not really interested' or 'I don't care'. It can sound quite negative and perhaps rude.
gonna wanna	*going to* is often pronounced in a shortened way as *gonna* /gənə/ or *gonte* /gɒntə/ *want* to is often pronounced *wanna* /wɒnə/ or *wanta* /wɒntə/
so	*so* is used before a verb to make it stronger. It has a meaning similar to *really* or *definitely*. It's often used before *not* + adjective or other negatives. *I'm so going to tell him what I think. = I'm definitely going to tell him what I think.* *I so don't like this food. = I really don't like this food.* *I so need to sleep. = I really need to sleep.* *That is so not clever. = That is definitely not clever.*

Remember! This is not 'exam' English!

1 'Translate' these sentences into standard English.

a We met at the bus stop and he was like, 'Where you going?'

We met at the bus stop and he said, 'Where are you going?'

b Kylie was like, 'What's your problem?'

....

c 'I so don't like this music.'

....

d The teacher goes, 'What you gonna do about this bad homework?'

....

e She was like, 'You wanna go into town?' and I was like, 'Whatever'.

....

2 **ABOUT YOU**

What do you think about the language in this unit?

- Is it a good idea to learn slang English?
- Or should you only focus on 'correct' English or 'exam' English?

Discuss these questions with a friend or with your teacher.

Irregular verbs

Infinitive	Past Simple	Past participle
be	was / were	been
become	became	become
begin	began	begun
bite	bit	bitten
break	broke	broken
bring	brought	brought
build	built	built
burn	burnt / burned	burnt / burned
buy	bought	bought
catch	caught	caught
choose	chose	chosen
come	came	come
cost	cost	cost
cut	cut	cut
do	did	done
draw	drew	drawn
drink	drank	drunk
drive	drove	driven
eat	ate	eaten
fall	fell	fallen
feed	fed	fed
feel	felt	felt
find	found	found
fly	flew	flown
forget	forgot	forgotten
freeze	froze	frozen
get	got	got
give	gave	given
go	went	gone / been
grow	grew	grown
have	had	had
hear	heard	heard
hide	hid	hidden
hit	hit	hit
hold	held	held
hurt	hurt	hurt
keep	kept	kept
know	knew	known
lay	laid	laid
learn	learnt / learned	learnt / learned
leave	left	left
lend	lent	lent

Infinitive	Past Simple	Past participle
lose	lost	lost
make	made	made
mean	meant	meant
meet	met	met
pay	paid	paid
put	put	put
read	read	read
ride	rode	ridden
ring	rang	rung
run	ran	run
say	said	said
see	saw	seen
set	set	set
sell	sold	sold
send	sent	sent
shine	shone	shone
shoot	shot	shot
show	showed	shown
shut	shut	shut
sing	sang	sung
sit	sat	sat
sleep	slept	slept
speak	spoke	spoken
spend	spent	spent
spill	spilt / spilled	spilt / spilled
split	split	split
stand	stood	stood
steal	stole	stolen
stick	stuck	stuck
swear	swore	sworn
swim	swam	swum
take	took	taken
teach	taught	taught
tear	tore	torn
tell	told	told
think	thought	thought
throw	threw	thrown
understand	understood	understood
wake	woke	woken
wear	wore	worn
win	won	won
write	wrote	written

Answer key

1 · I can ... Refer to people and things

1 **a** Harvard **b** coin, magazine **c** people, women
d art, furniture, money, music **e** coin, magazine, people, women

2 **b** them **c** us **d** it **e** him **f** me

3 **b** I've never seen <u>a necklace like this</u> before. It's so beautiful.

c <u>The snow</u> fell all night. When <u>Marty</u> woke up he ran to the window and stared out in amazement. It was everywhere.

d I love <u>the chocolate cakes</u> that you can buy in this bakery. They are just so delicious!

e We asked for some help with <u>the credit card problems</u> at the reception desk, but <u>the horrid man</u> said he couldn't do anything to help us with them.

f Keira and <u>her friends</u> got together and they decided to watch the <u>Wedding Disasters</u> DVD. But it didn't work.

2 · I can ... Make sentences with good word order

1 **b** Sue made <u>an Indian curry</u> for George.
c I'll give the children <u>five footballs</u>.
d The teacher lent me <u>his calculator</u>.
e The whole class saw <u>a fantastic film</u> at the cinema.
f Wendy bought her daughter <u>a new coat</u>.
g Wendy bought <u>a new coat</u> for her daughter.

2 **b** I'm repairing my car.
  S   V   O
c The teacher is asking the children for their homework.
   S   V   O   O
d Terry sent me a letter.
  S   V   O   O
e Gill will get us a cold drink.
  S   V   O   O
f Lenny wrote a short story for me.
  S   V   O   O

3 [Possible answers]
b a letter **c** a wonderful meal
d a new car **e** some questions about grammar

3 · I can ... Make simple descriptions

1 **b** salty **c** weekly **d** religious **e** sunny **f** famous
g dangerous / endangered **h** noisy **i** scientific **j** wonderful

2 **b** sleepy / sleeping / asleep **c** lost **d** shiny **e** written

3 **b** active **c** creative **d** breakable **e** fashionable **f** kissable
g attractive

4 **b** salty **c** bright **d** exhausted **e** educational **f** slippery
g blonde

4 · I can ... Use more than one adjective in my descriptions

1 **b** delicious Hungarian **c** long blonde **d** small, green, African
e boring, old, detective **f** nice, new, pink, German
g lovely and warm **h** horrible, long, black

2 **b** He's a friendly young tennis player.
c I bought a new Korean TV.
d We stared at the wonderful, ancient, stone statue.
e My mother has three lovely, large, round, ginger cats.
f Sandra played a pretty tune on some long, thin, bright red, metallic bells.

3 **b** a long red train **c** a large round lake **d** a fat brown cow
e a tall snowy mountain

5 · I can ... Talk about people's feelings and opinions

1 **b** annoying **c** surprised **d** relaxing **e** depressed
f interested **g** embarrassing **h** embarrassed **i** interesting
j interested

2 **b** 2 **c** 1 **d** 2 **e** 1 **f** 2 **g** 2

3 **b** **Mary:** Well, I'm glad you liked it. Jeff told me it was boring.
Beth: Seriously? He was bored? That's very ~~surprised~~ **surprising**.

c **Mary:** Yes. He was looking forward to it, but he said he was ~~disappointing~~ **disappointed**. He thought most of the magic tricks weren't very interesting.

d **Beth:** Well, I wasn't ~~boring~~ **bored** at all. The show was quite clever ... and very amusing as well. I laughed so much!

e **Beth:** One trick was really shocking! I was so ~~amazing~~ **amazed** when the giant rabbit jumped up!

4 Students' own answers

6 · I can ... Say how 'strong' something is

1 **b** I **totally** agree with everything that the managers said.
c The children are **terribly** tired.
d It's **rather** late. We need to go home.
e Priscilla has **almost** finished the gardening.
f We walked **fairly** quickly across the square to the ice cream shop.

2 **b** I hardly ever visit my grandma.
c Terry plays hockey a lot, but hardly ever plays football.
d I hardly ever drive a car.
e Jonah hardly ever leaves this village.

3 **b** This town has hardly changed since the 1960s.
c After going to the gym I can hardly move my legs!
d He is very shy and hardly talks to other children.

4 Students' own answers

7 · I can ... Talk about extremes

1 **b** very **c** absolutely **d** completely **e** really **f** totally
g absolutely **h** completely **i** very **j** totally **k** very
l absolutely

2 [Possible answers]
b freezing **c** impossible **d** terrifying / fantastic
e amazing / beautiful **f** unique **g** massive / enormous
h small / tiny

3 Students' own answers

8 · I can ... Make my descriptions more interesting

1 **b** Josie gave him <u>a huge box of expensive chocolates</u>.
c Could you pass me <u>that plate of red peppers</u>, please?
d What's <u>the answer to question 7</u>?
e <u>A very noisy car alarm</u> was going off all night.
f Giovanni won <u>the top prize for athletics</u> last September.

2 **b** him **c** them **d** her **e** it **f** They **g** us **h** It

3 **b** Kylie listened to the <u>beautiful classical</u> music <u>on Tom's headphones</u>.
c Mark cooked a <u>delicious</u> soup <u>full of fresh vegetables from the garden</u>.
d The children had a <u>fantastic two-week</u> holiday <u>at the seaside</u>.
e I flew here on a <u>rather frightening old</u> plane <u>with only two other passengers in it</u>.
f Caspar climbed to the top of a <u>tall</u> tree <u>on its own at the end of the park</u>.

Answer key

9 I can ... Describe actions

1 **b** In the morning, Michaela carefully cut the tall grass.
   c The lake water was icy, but we happily swam there for ten minutes.
   d You did a good job and deserved to win the prize!
   e This is my best jacket.
   f The early train arrived late.

2 **b** In the morning, Michaela carefully cut the tall grass.
   c The lake water was icy, but we happily swam there for ten minutes.
   d You worked well and deserved to win the prize!
   e I work best on my own.
   f The early train arrived late.

3 [Possible answers]
   b The ginger cat walked carefully along the top of the high brick wall. It stopped in front of the evergreen tree, then quickly jumped onto a low branch.
   c The lazy student looked anxiously at the exam questions. They seemed very difficult! She picked up her pen reluctantly and started to write neatly on the blank answer paper.

4 Students' own answers

10 I can ... Ask and answer about large quantities

1 **b** many **c** much **d** lots of **e** much **f** many **g** much
   h much **i** many **j** much **k** lots of **l** lots of

2 **b** How much money did Aunt Alma give the children?
   c How many sandwiches did you buy?
   d How much water did the climbers take with them to the camp?
   e How many water bottles did the climbers take with them to the camp?
   f How much tax did *InterWorld Shipping* pay last year?
   g How many cards did the boys sell for charity?
   h How much money did the boys make for charity?

11 I can ... Talk about different quantities

1 **b** 1 **c** 2 **d** 1 **e** 1 **f** 2 **g** 2

2 **b** A few (of the) eggs are broken.
   c All (of) the eggs aren't broken.
   d A couple of (the) eggs are broken.
   e None of the eggs are broken. No eggs are broken.
   f All (of) the eggs are broken.

3 **b** them **c** my **d** the **e** of **f** both **g** couple

12 I can ... Refer to things without repeating their name

1 **b** Is this computer better than that ~~computer~~ **one**?
   c These cakes are amazing! Which ~~cakes~~ **ones** do you want to take home?
   d This is the car park. My car is the red ~~car~~ **one** over there.
   e Ah look – this room has some ancient Egyptian statues. Yes, these are the ~~ancient Egyptian statues~~ **ones** the museum guidebook was talking about.
   f Are you having dancing lessons with Miss Gable? The ~~dancing lessons with Miss Gable~~ **ones** I went to last year were boring.
   g Did you buy a new phone charger? The ~~new phone chargers~~ **ones** I saw in the supermarket looked very poor quality – but the ~~new phone chargers~~ **ones** in the Dudley street market are really good. In fact, I bought ~~a new phone charger~~ **one** there myself! Would you like to get ~~a new phone charger~~ **one** now?

2 **c** blue one, yellow one **d** big one
   e pink ones **f** one with a cherry on top
   g one with fresh cream and one with strawberries

3 **c** I love those flowers. The purple ~~one~~ **ones** are so pretty!
   d There are twenty reports on the table. I want each person to take ~~ones~~ **one** and read it before the meeting.
   e My calculator has broken. Can I borrow ~~a~~ **one** from you?
   f Are you looking for laptop bags? I've got two ~~ones~~ next to my desk.

g It's not fair. Susie has got seven sweets, but I haven't got any ~~ones~~.

13 I can ... Talk about people/things when I don't know exactly who or what they are

1 **b** nothing **c** Nothing **d** Nobody **e** Nobody **f** nothing
   g nobody

2 **b** nobody **c** anybody **d** anybody
   e Nobody **f** nobody **g** anybody

3 **b** wants **c** is shouting **d** was **e** Has **f** happens
   g understands

4 **b** nothing **c** Someone **d** anything **e** Something **f** anybody

14 I can ... Name groups of people

1 **b** class **c** team **d** choir **e** crowd **f** government
   g department

2 Students' own answers

15 I can ... Say which person I'm talking about by saying what they are doing

1 **b** Person 5 **c** Person 7 **d** Person 1 **e** Person 6 **f** Person 2
   g Person 4

2 **b** the man drinking water / having a drink
   c the man knocking on the door
   d the man carrying the boxes
   e the woman eating a sandwich
   f the man throwing rubbish into the bin
   g the man holding a letter / giving a letter to the woman

16 I can ... Identify a person or thing by giving more information about them or it

1 **b** person who dances in the theatre
   c piece of metal that holds pieces of paper together
   d place where people borrow books
   e tool that cuts wood
   f famous person who wrote plays
   g cream that helps your skin
   h people who serve your food in a restaurant

2 [Possible answers]
   b A cinema is a place where you can watch films.
   c Mozart was a man who composed / wrote music.
   d An iPod is a thing that you can listen to music on.
   e An alien is something that lives in outer space.
   f A dishwasher is a machine that washes dishes.

3 **b** Jane Goodall was the woman who / that studied chimpanzees.
   c Joseph Priestley was the man who / that discovered oxygen.
   d The Eagle was the spaceship that took the first men to the Moon.
   e John Logie Baird was the man who / that invented TV.
   f Betsy Ross was the woman who / that made the first US flag.
   g The Kon-Tiki was the wooden ship that crossed the Pacific Ocean.

17 I can ... Identify a person by giving more information about them

1 **b** I met a girl who knew lots of pop stars.
   c The policeman who asked me lots of questions had a red badge.
   d We employed a plumber who had good recommendations.
   e Some guards who heard the alarm at 2 a.m. were working all night.
   f At the centre of the ancient temple we met a wise man who told us a secret.
   g The soldiers who were building the well worked all night.
   h Mariol got a text message from a boy who she met yesterday.

2 **b** who killed Julius Caesar
   c who invented the Caesar salad
   d who discovered the wreck of the Titanic
   e who took a historic bus ride
   f who sailed non-stop round the world

18 **I can … decide if it's possible to leave out** *who*

1 **b** In the middle of the car park I saw a woman **who** was sitting on top of her car!
  c Please pass the microphone to the man **who** put up his hand.
  d Harriet is an old lady **who** has lived in the hotel for more than 20 years.
  e I've met lots of people **who** really like the song.
  f People **who** live outside their own country often miss their favourite food.
  g That's the man Jane told us about.
  h This club was started by people **who** want to keep the old railway open.

2 **c** I'd like you to introduce to a man who / that parachuted off the Eiffel Tower!
  d I saw three people who / that were getting ready to play tennis.
  e Oh listen – this is the singer I recommended to our class last week.
  f The rescuers found a dog who / that survived the tornado.
  g This is the famous dog I wrote a newspaper article about.
  h These are the children I told a ghost story to.
  i The children who / that asked for a ghost story arrived early.

19 **I can … Say which thing I'm talking about**

1 **b** This is the train **that** goes to Glasgow.
  c This is a great smartphone app **that** counts all the calories in your food.
  d I can't stand cafés **that** have very loud music.
  e This is the CCTV camera **that** stopped working.
  f He sang a funny song about a dog **that** won first prize in a dog show.
  g What did you do with the money **that** Gabriela gave you?

2 **b** This is the report that I promised to write.
  c Here are the second-hand toys that Marilyn gave to the nursery.
  d Did you watch the TV programme that had a million-dollar prize?
  e The apples that you bought last week are bad.
  f Has anyone seen the glove that I left here this morning?
  g All the work that we did was useless.
  h The lake that is in the middle of the park is beautiful.

3 [Possible answers] **b** a ruler **c** a car **d** an elephant

4 [Possible answers]
  b something that is made of glass
  c something that you wear on your foot
  d something that you can do sums with

5 Students' own answers

20 **I can … Compare things**

1 **b** happier **c** the most exciting **d** wider **e** bad
  f the worst **g** the least popular **h** wetter **i** the wettest
  j good **k** better **l** more attractive **m** the most attractive
  n fewer **o** the fewest **p** nicer **q** the nicest **r** busier
  s the busiest **t** closer **u** the closest

2 **b** smaller **c** tastier **d** more exciting **e** more crowded
  f older **g** darker

3 **b** the untidiest room **c** the most expensive thing
  d the least successful student **e** the rainiest summer
  f the hottest summer **g** the most horrible noise

21 **I can … Say that some things are 'less' than others**

1 **c** Box X isn't as expensive as Box Y. **d** Box X is older than Box Y.
  e Box Y is taller than Box X. **f** Box X isn't as bright as Box Y.
  g Box X is colder than Box Y. **h** Box Y isn't as damaged as Box X.

2 **b** *The Little Prince* isn't as long as *War and Peace*.
  c Your dinner is tastier than my dinner.
  d Mike didn't answer as many questions as Sophie.
  e My old phone was better than my new one.
  f This week, class 6A's work wasn't as bad as class 6B's work.

3 **b** The Panama Canal isn't as long as the Suez Canal.
  c Panthers aren't as fast as cheetahs.
  d Machu Picchu isn't as old as Great Zimbabwe.
  e The Arctic isn't as cold as the Antarctic.

22 **I can … Say that things are similar**

1 **b** I work as hard as you!
  c I do my homework as carefully as you.
  d I get up as early as you on Saturdays.
  e My school's as big as yours.
  f My dad plays the guitar as brilliantly as your dad.

2 **b** 4 **c** 1 **d** 5 **e** 6 **f** 3

23 **I can … Emphasise the meaning of adjectives**

1 **b** strange **c** strangely **d** stupid **e** generous **f** generous
  g generously **h** noisily **i** suddenly **j** well **k** good

2 **b** so cheap **c** so glad **d** so keen **e** so sad **f** so tiring, so hilly

3 **b** That cake was so delicious that I ate three slices!
  c The Biology exam was so difficult that I couldn't finish it.
  d I'm sorry I can't help you this morning. I'm so busy that I don't have any free time.
  e The song became so popular that everyone was singing it.
  f When he thought about the trip he became so anxious that he cancelled it.
  g The family was so poor that they could only afford soup for dinner.

4 **b** such a boring opera **c** such a strong man
  d such a difficult question **e** such a spicy meal
  f such a ridiculous story

24 **I can … Say that there is more of something than is good**

1 **b** too narrow **c** too expensive, too poor **d** too far
  e too tired **f** too dark

2 **b** too few cakes **c** too many passengers **d** too little time
  e too much noise **f** too few seats **g** too much work

3 **b** They were too lazy to finish the work.
  c This river is too dangerous to swim in.
  d The owner is too ill to see you.
  e Martin is too shy to talk to Jane.
  f I'm too embarrassed to say what I did.

25 **I can … Say that there is less of something than is good**

1 **b** didn't have enough money **c** didn't have enough onions
  d didn't have enough time **e** didn't have enough space / room in her car **f** didn't have enough ideas

2 **b** not intelligent enough **c** not hot enough **d** not tall enough
  e not confident enough **f** not rich enough **g** not well enough

3 Students' own answers

26 **I can … Talk about things I am interested in**

1 **b** by **c** about **d** of **e** with **f** by **g** on **h** about **i** about
  j with

2 **b** serious about **c** surprised by **d** shocked by
  e interested in **f** hopeful about **g** curious about
  h capable of **i** shocked by **j** satisfied with **k** delighted with

3 Students' own answers

27 **I can … Describe people's characters**

1 **b** of **c** at **d** to **e** at **f** about **g** to **h** of **i** for **j** of

2 Students' own answers

28 **I can … Express my emotional reactions**

1 **b** about **c** about / with **d** of **e** with **f** with **g** of **h** about
  i with **j** about

2 **b** Bo was nervous about taking his test.
  c He was disappointed about the result.
  d He was happy about the result.
  e He was excited about driving.
  f He was angry about the theft.

29 **I can … Describe how people behave to each other**

1 **b** of **c** to **d** of **e** to **f** of **g** of **h** to

2 [Possible answers]
  b a lovely meal / a delicious meal / a tasty meal

Answer key

c   a fantastic view / a beautiful view / a stunning view
d   an interesting museum / a fascinating museum / a wonderful museum
e   a lovely song / a tuneful song / a catchy song
f   helpful / friendly / professional
g   cool / refreshing / deep
h   a sunny day / a hot day / a beautiful day

(30) I can ... Say how I travelled and where I stayed

1   b   by bike   c   in my car   d   in an ambulance
    e   by high-speed train   f   on foot   g   by ferry   h   by air
2   b   on   c   in   d   at   e   in   f   by, by   g   on
3   Students' own answers

(31) I can ... Talk about work and work problems

1   b   of   c   of   d   for   e   of   f   of   g   for   h   of
2   b   types of   c   reason for   d   jpeg of   e   disadvantages of
    f   time for   g   respect for
3   b   of the King   c   of her exams yet   d   of her accident
    e   of spare parts   f   for her son's strange behaviour

(32) I can ... Talk about working with difficult people

1   b   5   c   1   d   2   e   4
2   b   Sean has never had a good relationship **with** his father.
    c   Are the boys having any problems **with** their new teacher?
    d   Did I have a conversation about the new computers **with** you yesterday? I can't remember.
    e   Every summer we spend time in the countryside **with** our children.
3   Students' own answers

(33) I can ... Talk about what I do online

1   b   with   c   for   d   for   e   about   f   about   g   through   h   with
2   c   I spent all afternoon uploading with my holiday photos. ✗
    d   Oh Kelly! Tell me that you didn't really join to the new BestFace forum! ✗
    e   Did you make friends with those new members? ✓
    f   I've looked everywhere for my password – but I can't find it! ✓
    g   Hey, everyone. I've just posted up a new message on my blog. ✗
    h   Ted spent five minutes looking at the picture, but he couldn't find me in it! ✓
    i   Could you email the director's contact details to me, please? ✓

(34) I can ... Recognise verbs in different forms

1   b   The children are going to eat lunch in the garden.
    c   She's been to New Delhi.
    d   What are you going to do about it?
    e   The soldiers were driving too fast.
    f   Trudie's answering the phone right now.
2   b   8   c   1   d   3   e   6   f   5   g   7   h   2
3   a   watched   b   watched   c   fly   d   flew   e   begin   f   begun
    g   go   h   gone / been   i   draw   j   drew   k   fall   l   fallen   m   felt
    n   felt   o   caught   p   caught   q   choose   r   chosen   s   forget
    t   forgot   u   knew   v   known   w   meant   x   meant   y   hurt
    z   hurt

(35) I can ... Talk about situations that are changing

1   b   is getting   c   is becoming   d   is expanding
    e   are building   f   is getting
2   b   The internet is changing all the time.
    c   My English marks are getting better.
    d   The cost of living is increasing.
    e   Mobile phone charges are rising again.
    f   The population is getting older.

(36) I can ... Use present tenses

1   b   are   c   don't   d   does   e   ask   f   have   g   think   h   Am
    i   having   j   asking   k   thinking

2   b   1   Present Progressive   2   future – at the end of the month
    c   1   Present Simple   2   future
    d   1   Present Progressive   2   present
    e   1   Present Simple   2   future
    f   1   Present Simple   2   past, present and future – repeated event
3   b   wants   c   are arriving   d   goes   e   is reading
    f   are working   g   doesn't believe
4   b   finish   c   changes   d   is starting   e   doesn't like   f   works
    g   is working   h   is speaking   i   speaks   j   talks   k   is talking

(37) I can ... Talk about events in the past

1   b   Present Perfect   c   Past Progressive   d   Past Simple
    e   Past Progressive   f   Present Perfect   g   Past Progressive
    h   Past Simple   i   Past Simple, Past Progressive
    j   Past Simple, Past Simple, Past Simple
    k   Past Progressive, Past Simple   l   Past Progressive, Past Progressive   m   Present Perfect   n   Past Simple, Past Simple, Past Progressive
2   b   've told, did you tell   c   've been, did they go
    d   made, were they doing   e   caught, did they catch
    f   've broken, have they / has broken   g   bought, Have you driven   h   has bitten, Did you annoy
3   c   went   d   were playing   e   met, was doing   f   have you seen
    g   Did you enjoy   h   swam   i   was swimming, saw
    j   were taking, were marking / marked   k   has just knocked over

(38) I can ... Give a general idea about when something happened

1   b   immediately   c   earlier   d   eventually   e   recently
2   b   already   c   yet   d   yet   e   still   f   already   g   yet   h   still
3   [Possible answers]   c   I did it earlier.   d   I'm still doing it.
    e   I've already done it.   f   I went there recently.
    g   I met him / her previously.

(39) I can tell an interesting story about my life

1   b   Past Progressive   c   Present Simple   d   Past Simple
    e   Past Simple   f   Present Perfect   g   Present Simple
    h   Past Simple   i   Present Simple
2   b   was working   c   died   d   was   e   called   f   have you tried
    g   'm panicking   h   Have you made   i   don't know   j   mended
    k   asked   l   said   m   got
3   Students' own answers

(40) I can ... Ask how long someone has been doing something

1   b   How long has Peter been working here?
    c   How long has she been going out with Tim?
    d   What has she been doing?
    e   Where has he been staying?
    f   Has he been cooking all evening?
    g   Have they been playing video games for three hours?
    h   Who has Sarah been working with?
2   c   How long have they been watching TV?
    d   What has Jenny been cooking?
    e   Where has he been hiding?
    f   Has Jamie been living in Spain?
    g   Have you been playing football?
    h   How long have those young men been looking for work?
3   [Possible answers]
    How long has Joanna been waiting?
    What have Joanna and her father been looking for?
    What have they been celebrating?
    Where has Joanna been staying?
    Where have they been celebrating?
    Where have they been looking?
    Who has Joanna been looking for?
    Who have they been waiting for?
    Why has her father been waiting?

41 **I can emphasise the length of time of an action**

1 b We've been talking all night.
   c I've been waiting for you since this morning!
   d Our new cheese hasn't been selling very well.
   e It's been working well all year.

2 b The baby's been playing for four hours.
   c They've been working in our street for four days.
   d Helen's been studying at Dance College for seven months.
   e They've been painting the kitchen wall for twenty minutes.
   f Hugh's been working at Dekker Furniture for 29 years.

3 b Keith's been singing for one hour.
   c You've been wearing the same shirt for five days!
   d I've been asking you since yesterday afternoon.
   e I've been thinking about the problem for seven days.
   f We've been playing cards since midnight / for four hours!
   g Lara's been sleeping since lunchtime.

42 **I can … Talk about things I did in the past (but not now)**

1 b used to study Geography c used to read thrillers
   d used to eat fast food e used to go to the cinema
   f used to buy CDs g used to be a cleaner
   h used to have twenty

2 b did she use to study? c did he use to be?
   d did you use to live? e did she use to go?
   f did she use to come / travel / get to work?
   g did she use to date? h did he use to read?

3 b used to work c used to take d didn't use to drive
   e used to go f didn't use to have g used to read
   h used to ride

4 Students' own answers

43 **I can … Explain that one thing happened before another**

1 b	**2**	When I arrived,	**1**	Tim had already been to the shops.
c	1	I'd already printed six photos	2	when I noticed the problem.
d	1	He'd learnt Spanish	2	by the time he was 18.
e	2	When the guard returned,	1	the man had escaped.
f	1	Jemima had just come in	2	when the fire alarm rang.
g	2	My mother was really surprised	1	that we had made her a birthday cake.
h	1	Shelley had asked for a tea,	2	but they gave her a coffee.

2 b had left c had landed d had heard e had gone
   f had sailed g had been h had had

3 b my phone rang c the football match had already started
   d her computer crashed e had just scored a goal
   f Mia came home

44 **I can … Talk about things I noticed, realised, saw, etc.**

1 b I heard from my friends that Miranda had left Sri Lanka.
   c We read on the website that the new dresses had all sold out in a few minutes.
   d The examiner noticed that someone had changed the photo on the girl's identity card.
   e I realised that Meg had driven the whole way.
   f I noticed that Carla had gone.
   g I saw that someone had eaten all the food.
   h I heard that Chip had chosen the Physics course.

2 [Possible answers]
   b had sacked him by text c had burgled it / broken in
   d had beaten Manchester United

45 **I can … Explain reasons for past events**

1 b Because they'd caught flu.
   c Because she'd failed her / the exam.
   d Because he'd heard lots of ghost stories!

   e Because he'd seen the first twenty minutes.
   f Because she'd found one she really liked.

46 **I can … Set the 'start time' of a story**

1 b The managers arrived. The secretary had already prepared everything.
   c We said hello to Rufus at Julian's party. We had already seen him at the office.
   d Jane called Zak's mobile. Zak had already tried to call the office.
   e We came in at 8 o'clock. The thieves had already taken all the microchips and left.
   f The party went on till midnight. Sylvia had already gone home.

2 She had hidden behind a tree and watched him. He had taken his phone out of his jacket and called a number. She had heard his message and written it down. She had watched him leave.

3 b written, plays c the Moon, been d Victoria, discovered, the West Indies e an Oscar, lost f the Great Eastern, built

47 **I can … Say that something happened before a certain time**

1 b had blown c had cooked d had gone e had had
   f had left g had woken up

2 [Possible answers]
   b had done five tests c had finished work
   d had eaten a lot of food e had waited for two hours

48 **I can … Make Past Perfect negatives**

1 b She hadn't arrived. c He hadn't found it yet.
   d They hadn't flown before. e They hadn't done it.
   f I hadn't bought it yet.

2 [Possible answers]
   Nick had never been to the capital.
   Nick hadn't met Rose before.
   Nick hadn't seen the film before.
   Rose had never met Nick before.
   Rose had forgotten Nick had never been to the capital.

49 **I can … Talk about the future**

1 b are c going d will e will f going / flying / travelling
   g won't h watch i will

2 b I'll / be c 'll / show d is going to order e 'm working
   f it's going to rain g it'll stop

3 [Possible answers]
   I will meet you at 3 o'clock.
   I'll meet you at the stadium at 3 o'clock.
   I'm going to visit you next month.
   It might rain tomorrow.
   It's going to rain.
   Matthew might visit her next month.
   Matthew's going to play football tomorrow.
   Matthew's going to visit her on Saturday.
   You might meet Matthew tomorrow.
   You're going to play football tomorrow.

50 **I can talk about timetabled events**

1 c close d start e get f last g closes h starts i last
   j gets

2 b gets c leaves d stop / call e take f arrives
   g starts / begins h starts / begins i lasts

51 **I can … Talk about things that will possibly happen**

1 Students' own answers

2 b I might watch a film or I may bake a cake.
   c She might be in the garden or she may not be at home.
   d He might make a pizza or he may not cook anything!
   e He might have a cold or he may be stressed because of his work.
   f He might borrow a suit or he may buy a cheap one from a second-hand shop.

3 [Possible answers]
   He might drop the boxes. It might rain.
   The cyclists might crash. The dog might steal some meat.

Answer key

The man on the roof might fall down.
The paint might fall on someone's head.
The old couple might go into the shop.

(52) I can ... Make *yes/no* questions in different tenses

1 **c** Do they play computer games after school? Present Simple
d Are they going to practise in the gym? *be going to*
e Were the visitors waiting for me? Past Progressive
f Has she flown to Washington? Present Perfect
g Did he catch a train to Brighton? Past Simple
h Does she like pasta? Present Simple

2 **c** Was John having a shower?
d Did your mum book her plane tickets online?
e Do the engineers work every day?
f Have they visited Australia?
g Did you feel cold?
h Is that plane going to take off?
i Have the chickens woken up?

(53) I can ... Make *Wh-* questions

1 **c** Why was Jake crying? **d** Who's going to cook lunch?
e Who flew to Las Vegas? **f** What have they stolen?
g When did she write her blog post?
h What does Greg eat for lunch? **i** Who has Tom spoken to?
j Who has spoken to Tom? **k** Who did Tom speak to?
l Who spoke to Tom?

2 **c** Why did you go there? **d** What did you discover?
e What did it look like? **f** What was it doing when you found it?
g What did you do with it? **h** Where does it live now?
i How long has she been there? **j** What's making that noise?
k What is she going to do to us? / What will she do to us?
l How do you know?

(54) I can ... Ask questions when I think I know the answer

1 **b** The boys were late, weren't they?
c You didn't buy a new hat, did you?
d These books are exciting, aren't they?
e He's got a discount ticket, hasn't he?
f We went there last summer, didn't we?
g You're not the new accountant, are you?
h I'm player number one, aren't I?

2 **b** This is the right way, isn't it?
c The clean towels are in the drawer, aren't they?
d The car was parked outside, wasn't it?
e He is going to make the cakes, isn't he?
f They left the show early, didn't they?
g The lessons weren't cancelled, were they?

3 **b** You bought some bread, didn't you?
c The printers were all damaged, weren't they?
d The printers are all damaged, aren't they?
e The printer isn't damaged, is it?
f ✓

(55) I can ... Ask questions more politely

1 **b** Do you know where the train station is?
c Excuse me. Could you tell me when this shop closes?
d I was wondering if / whether you enjoyed your holiday.
e Would you mind telling me what mark Alice got?
f Can you tell me if / whether the meeting finished successfully?
g I wonder if you know whether the CEO wants everyone at the meeting.
h May I ask you what subject you studied at university?

2 [Possible answers]
b Excuse me. Could you tell me the football score?
c Excuse me. Would you mind telling me if I passed the test?
e Excuse me. I wonder if you know when the next bus is due.
f Have you got any idea if it's a boy or a girl?
g Excuse me. I was wondering if I could look at the newspaper.

3 [Possible answers]
Could you tell me what her name is?
Do you know what her name is?
I don't know if you know her name.

I was wondering if you could tell me what your name is.
I wonder if you know my name.
I wonder if you know what her name is.

(56) I can ... Report what people said

1 **b** She said that she was getting ready for the children's party.
c She said that she wanted to make some decorations.
d She said that she didn't feel tired.
e She said that the garden looked beautiful.
f She said that she wasn't organising any games.
g She said that she hoped that Mark liked the hot weather.

2 **b** 'I agree with the Prime Minister's decision.'
c 'I enjoy my work.'
d 'I am waiting for more information.'
e 'I don't believe in Father Christmas.'
f 'I am resigning next week.'

(57) I can ... Report people's ideas about the future

1 **b** the team was going to be late.
c he might go to London.
d the plane would arrive soon.
e the children were going to listen to some music.
f the computer might not work.

2 **c** 'm going to be very **d** plan will go
e will think of a better **f** 've got a new
g 'm going to pretend to be
h will hear me and come in to our prison
i will run out quickly and lock the
j 'll be trapped in the cell with the
k 'll come back to rescue you

3 **b** We will remember not the words of our enemies, but the silence of our friends. Martin Luther King
c I will let you be in my dreams if I can be in yours. Bob Dylan

(58) I can ... Report people's stories about past events

1 **b** He said he'd / he's watched a great DVD.
c He said he'd never seen a 3D film before.
d He said it was / had been great.
e He said he forgot / had forgotten to check the news about the Oscars.
f He said he went / had been to the film premiere.
g He said that he said / had said hello to Jason Isaacs.

2 **b** He said that they had chosen really interesting topics.
c He said that the students had never done anything like it before.
d He said that he thought that the results were high quality.
e He said that some students had displayed their projects in the school hall.
f He said that he liked the one about volcanoes most.

(59) I can ... Choose the correct reporting verb

1 **b** told **c** said **d** told **e** said **f** told **g** said
2 **b** told **c** said **d** told **e** tell **f** say **g** say **h** told **i** said

(60) I can ... Report people's questions

1 **b** 'Why is the bridge shut?' **c** 'Who is the man?'
d 'Do you like chips?' **e** 'Where is your group working?'
f 'Are you planning to make dinner?' **g** 'Is my / his painting good?'
h 'Can you help me?'

2 **b** Debbie asked me what the time was.
c Judy asked me where the cats went / had gone.
d Sam asked me if I liked garlic.
e Ted asked me who my doctor was.
f Marc asked me when the children left / had left.
g Susie asked me if I wanted some apple pie.
h Mick asked me if I could play the guitar.

(61) I can ... Say what people thought

1 **b** it was a great party **c** the children were happy
d it was the wrong answer **e** her team was going to win
f it was too cold to go out **g** she would buy a new chair

2 Students' own answers

(62) I can ... Say how people spoke in different ways

1 b announced that he would resign the next day
   c explained that he couldn't eat sweets all day as they are bad for you
   d whispered that he loved her
   e announced that the shopping centre was closing at 8 o'clock
   f explained that the word 'location' meant 'place'
   g complained that the flat was very dirty
   h whispered that he needed to go to the toilet

2 b complained c replied d whispered

(63) I can ... State facts that are always or generally true

1 b 4 c 5 d 2 e 1
2 b 4 c 1 d 5 e 3
3 b 5 c 1 d 2 e 4
4 b Water boils c DVD rewinds d recording starts
   e snow melts f car stops g eyes, see

(64) I can ... Tell people what to do if something happens

1 b refill the tank c put on your warm hat and scarf
   d call your doctor immediately e put a cartoon film on for them
   f try again

2 [Possible answers]
   b leave the building immediately c call reception
   d take it off the heat e leave them for a while f give it to him

(65) I can ... Say what will happen when another thing happens

1 b I'll read the book before I will watch the film.
   c After you will phone Terry we can go out.
   d Marty will tell you about the meeting when you will come into the office.
   e Susie will wait until I will finish this job.
   f I'll buy you a present when you will tell me what you want!

2 b takes off, will be c is, will call d will wait, finishes
   e will pay, send f will be, close g will introduce, starts
   h will be, arrives i will catch, starts

(66) I can ... Say what will happen if another thing happens

1 b When c if d if e If
2 b If we will arrive before midday, we'll have lunch with Greig.
   c Mac will check the database if you'll ask him.
   d If all the children will come into the classroom, Mrs Morris will explain the plan.
   e If we will hurry, we'll be at the theatre in time.
   f I'll tidy the chairs if you will move the tables.

3 b comes, will make c will fall down, put d snows, will cancel
   e gets, will call f will tell, ask g buy, will you do

(67) I can ... Give warnings, advice, predictions, threats and promises

1 b 'll help, get c 'll come, promise d change, will give
   e need, will explain

2 b can, go c will send, write d will help, ask
   e book, will save f lock, will be

(68) I can ... Imagine an unlikely or impossible present or future

1 b If I got a job, I'd start saving.
   c You'd pay less if you went to a bed and breakfast hotel.
   d If our team lost to Portsmouth, we'd be out of the competition.
   e We could get to the finals if we won against Barcelona
   f If everyone gave 10% of their income, we'd feed the whole world.
   g If you found €100 in the street, would you report it to the police?

2 b If I wanted it, I'd eat it.
   c If I understood it, I'd do it.

d If I had some money, I'd lend it to you.
e If I believed you, I'd be frightened!

(69) I can ... Ask about unlikely futures

1 b became c won d had e were f needed
   g discovered, had h told, cheated

2 b What would you do if there was a big earthquake?
   c What would you think if I reduced salaries by 10% next year?
   d What would you say if I found a spy from a rival company?
   e What would you recommend if I wanted to save $20 million?

(70) I can ... Give advice by saying what I would do

1 b 'd work c 'd tell d 'd rewrite e 'd do

2 b If I were you, I'd become an English teacher. / I'd become an English teacher if I were you.
   c If I were you, I'd get a telescope. / I'd get a telescope if I were you.
   d If I were you, I'd eat less chocolate. / I'd eat less chocolate if I were you.
   e If I were you, I'd book some lessons. / I'd book some lessons if I were you.

3 b If I were you, I'd visit Frankfurt. / I'd visit Frankfurt if I were you.
   c If I were you, I'd phone her right now. / I'd phone her right now if I were you.
   d If I were you, I wouldn't argue. / I wouldn't argue if I were you.
   e If I were you, I'd go straight home. / I'd go straight home if I were you.

(71) I can ... Give people advice about specific problems

1 b 6 c 4 d 7 e 2 f 8 g 1 h 5

2 [Possible answers]
   b You'd better go to bed early tonight.
   c You'd better put on a jumper.
   d You'd better find something to do.
   e You'd better apologise to him.
   f You'd better take a painkiller.
   g You'd better run!
   h You'd better buy yourself a sandwich.
   i You'd better call him / her now.

(72) I can ... Say how I am prepared for possible events

1 b 5 c 1 d 6 e 2 f 4

2 [Possible answers]
   b I'll take an umbrella in case it rains.
   c I'll take the car in case the trains aren't running.
   d I'll make a vegetable dish in case any of my guests are vegetarian.
   e I'll tell my mum to call me in case my alarm doesn't ring.
   f I'll record *Celebrity Shoes* in case I don't get home till 8.30.

3 a 3 b 2 c 1

(73) I can ... Describe processes and routines

1 b is printed c are designed d is stored e are connected
   f is served g is recorded h is repainted

2 b are cleaned c are opened d is staffed e are made
   f is asked g is closed, locked

3 b 6 c 1 d 7 e 2 f 5 g 4

4 Students' own answers

(74) I can ... Talk about historical facts

1 b The novel *Pride and Prejudice* was written by Jane Austen.
   c The inside of the Statue of Liberty was designed by Gustave Eiffel.
   d The character of Batman was created by Bob Kane.
   e Penicillin was discovered by Alexander Fleming.
   f The first iPad was launched in 2010.
   g England was invaded in 1066.

2 b When was the first Barbie doll made?
   c Where were the first Olympic Games held?
   d Which film was awarded the 'Best Picture' Oscar in 2012?
   e When was the first mobile phone demonstrated?

f Where were *The Lord of the Rings* and *The Hobbit* filmed?

g When was the first tweet sent?

h What was discovered in Egypt in 1922?

3 a 1963 **b** 1959 **c** Greece **d** *The Artist* **e** 1973
   f New Zealand **g** 2006 **h** Tutankhamen's tomb

4 b were given **c** was checked **d** were searched
   e were caught **f** were shot **g** were opened
   h were held **i** was pulled down **j** was reunited

(75) ## I can ... Ask if we are ready for an event

1 b Mark **c** Julie **d** Julie **e** Mark **f** Mark **g** Julie **h** Julie

2 b been washed **c** been wrapped **d** been put up
   e been turned on **f** been decorated **g** been sent **h** been told

(76) ## I can ... Avoid saying who did something

1 b The report has been lost.
   c The room has been tidied.
   d The newspapers were torn.
   e The jewellery has been stolen.
   f Mark Andrews was elected.
   g Pat has been sacked.
   h All the food was eaten.
   i The lecture has been interrupted.

2 b was printed by the local newspaper
   c was drawn by my two-year-old daughter
   d were made by the managing directors
   e were baked by my mother
   f were won by our local team

3 b The chemicals have been collected from the fridge.
   c The windows have been shut and the lights have been switched off.
   d Lots of questions have been asked on the blog.
   e An answer for this problem has never been found.

(77) ## I can ... Talk about something unexpected that happened

1 b got left behind **c** got lost **d** got mixed up **e** got flooded
   f got paid

2 c We got invited to a terrible party.
   d We got arrested.
   e We got released six hours later!
   f Jorge got asked for some money.
   g Our flight back got cancelled.
   h Our luggage got sent to the wrong airport.

(78) ## I can ... Use the passive in different tenses

1 b The password has been changed.
   c Lunch is being prepared.
   d The exam results will be sent next week.
   e The alarm was being repaired.
   f The gate wasn't closed properly.
   g The wedding is going to be cancelled.

2 b The boat was ~~steal~~ **stolen** after midnight.
   c The concert hall **is** going to be redecorated next month.
   d The DVD player and the TV ~~was~~ **were** broken.
   e The customer's order is ~~been~~ **being** packed in those large boxes over there.
   f Don't panic! The missing tiger will be ~~find~~ **found**!
   g The essays were ~~be~~ **being** marked in the staff room.
   h That film will never be ~~show~~ **shown** in our country.

3 c It's being washed. **d** He was being changed.
   e It's being cooked. **f** They were being used.
   g They are being filmed. **h** They were being attacked.

4 b Our TV has been stolen! Reason (ii)
   c That tourist was given the wrong information. Reason (i)
   d Graffiti was sprayed on the old fountain. Reason (ii)
   e The office will be cleaned after the party. Reason (ii)
   f Heavy metal music was being played much too loud. Reason (i)
   g The Minister's speech is going to be interrupted. Reason (ii)
   h They were searched at the airport. Reason (ii)

(79) ## I can ... Decide which 'had' is which

1 b 3 **c** 2 **d** 2 **e** 1 **f** 2

2 b The actors had new costumes.
   The actors had made new costumes.
   The actors had had new costumes.
   c Marina had three magazines.
   Marina had delivered three magazines.
   Marina had had three magazines.
   d Susie had expensive black shoes
   Suzie had cleaned her expensive black shoes.
   Suzie had had expensive black shoes.

3 a **2** Anne had a new boss. **3** The boss had lunch.
   b **2** Anne had printed the report. **3** Anne had repaired the printer.

4 b would **c** had **d** would **e** would **f** had **g** had **h** would

(80) ## I can ... Talk about things people did themselves

1 b herself **c** themselves **d** yourself **e** ourselves

2 b looked, herself **c** enjoy themselves **d** helped themselves
   e let yourself **f** taught myself **g** blame myself
   h set yourself **i** threw himself

(81) ## I can ... say that someone did something (and not another person)

1 b wrote it all by myself **c** broke it myself **d** found it myself
   e scored it myself **f** bought it myself

2 b himself **c** myself **d** themselves **e** ourselves **f** yourselves

(82) ## I can ... Think about facts and make an intelligent guess

1 b It must be a ghost. **c** It must be a sci-fi film.
   d It must be a joke. **e** He must be a detective.

2 b It must be Susan. ✓
   ~~It can't be Susan.~~
   ~~It must be Mike.~~
   It can't be Mike. ✓
   ~~It must be Lou.~~
   c ~~She can't be a good teacher.~~
   She must be a good teacher. ✓
   ~~She must be a bad teacher.~~
   ~~She must be a noisy teacher.~~

(83) ## I can ... Talk about things that are necessary to do

1 b 1 **c** 6 **d** 2 **e** 4 **f** 5

2 c had to ✓ / must ✗ **d** have to ✓ / need to ✓
   e need to ✗ / must ✓ **f** have to ✓ / had to ✗

3 b has to **c** have to **d** had to **e** have to **f** Do, have to
   g Do, have to

4 b 3 b **c** 3 c **d** 3 e

(84) ## I can ... Talk about things that it is important not to do

1 Students' own answers

2 b mustn't forget **c** mustn't fail **d** mustn't stay
   e mustn't lose **f** mustn't break

(85) ## I can ... Talk about things that aren't necessary

1 b You don't have to pay anything.
   c You don't have to come earlier.
   d You don't have to decide now.
   e You don't have to pay in cash.
   f You don't have to re-enter your password.
   g You don't have to apologise.

2 b don't have to **c** mustn't **d** don't have to **e** mustn't
   f mustn't **g** don't have to

(86) ## I can ... Talk about past actions that weren't necessary

1 b It's good that you didn't come to work this morning. You didn't need to be / ~~needn't have been~~ at the 8 o'clock meeting.
   c She gave her hairdresser a £10 tip! Why? She didn't need to do that / needn't have done that. ✓
   d Olga took the train to Moscow. She didn't need to fly / ~~needn't have flown~~.

e I got home at 2 a.m. My parents waited up until I came back! They didn't need to do that / needn't have done that! ✔

f Why did you stop our football game? You didn't need to stop / needn't have stopped it so early! ✔

2 b You needn't have worried about Judy.
c You needn't have borrowed £2,000 from the bank.
d You needn't have queued for ten hours to buy a concert ticket.
e You needn't have studied all night for the Science exam!
f You needn't have taken your laptop to work.

3 a 1 b 1 c 1

(87) I can … Use *can, could* and *should*

1 b Can / Could c couldn't d can't e couldn't f can't
g couldn't h Can / Could

2 [Possible answers]
b You should go to bed immediately.
c You should go to the doctor.
d You should try to learn ten English words every day.
e You should give the last piece of pizza to your mum.

3 b 1 c 5 d 2 e 6 f 4

4 b you're right
c we must first believe that we can
d but everyone can help someone
e it's day-to-day living that wears you out
f if I could do all I can?
g it can only become stairs

(88) I can … Talk about past and future abilities

1 c We were able to solve a problem with the antenna.
d We were able to go to a conference in Dubai.
e We were able to meet lots of programmers from around the world.
f We couldn't find a way to make it more economically.
g We were able to improve the software.

2 c I could cook a great meal for Benny when he came round yesterday. ✗
I was able to cook a great meal for Benny when he came round yesterday.
d I could run quite fast until I broke my leg last year. ✔
e I could watch the video when I was on my lunch break. ✗
I was able to watch the video when I was on my lunch break.
f When I was a teenager I could beat anybody at online racing games. ✔

3 b was able to c were able to d can / am able to
e 'll be able to

4 Students' own answers

(89) I can … Talk about things which were possible, but didn't happen

1 c Oh, Sandra! You could have asked for help.
d Oh, Mary! You could have come on time.
e Oh, Tommy! You could have bought some cakes for the party.
f Oh, Jo! You could have left your dog at home.
g Oh, Jenny! You could have made your bed.

2 [Possible answers]
b I could have caught the bus.
I could have stayed at home.
I could have brought an umbrella.
c I could have studied harder.
I could have gone to all my classes.
I could have done some practice tests.
d I could have stayed at home last night.
I could have left the party earlier.
I could have phoned in sick this morning.
e I could have bought a cheaper car.
I could have bought a bus pass instead.
I could have bought a bicycle.
f I could have looked online for an instruction video.
I could have asked for some help.
I could have paid a professional to do it.

3 b couldn't have gone c couldn't have known
d couldn't have explained e couldn't have imagined

(90) I can … Tell the story of an adventure

1 b forgot to tell c agreed to give d need to explain
e offered to lend f hope to see g learnt to drive
h agreed to help i threatened to throw

2 b started to look for / started looking for c began to discuss / began discussing d decided to fly e try to travel
f hoped to see g have forgotten to do h refuse to allow
i expected to stay

3 Students' own answers

(91) I can … Talk about things I like and dislike doing

1 b playing c seeing d watching e doing f reading
g smoking h having i telling j winning k getting
l missing m trying

2 b finished painting c gave up teaching
d suggested meeting e is looking forward to seeing
f admitted driving g don't mind eating
h prefer making / prefer to make

(92) I can … Use *remember* and *stop*

1 c ✔ d ✔ e ✗ f ✔ g ✗ h ✗ i ✔ j ✔ k ✔ l ✗
m ✔ n ✔

2 Students' own answers

(93) I can … Use *forget, try* and *manage to*

1 b to make c walking d to get e watching f to call
g to live / living h to mend i changing

2 Students' own answers

(94) I can … Describe conversations with other people

1 b to c to d Ø e about f for g about h at i with
j about k with l Ø m for n Ø, Ø

2 c Ø d to e for f to g about h Ø i about

(95) I can … Use *get* with different meanings

1 b became c arrived somewhere d received e became
f took a vehicle g arrived somewhere h bought / paid for
i arrived somewhere

2 b Marisa said she'll get lunch for everyone.
c I hope we can get the 10.25 train or we'll be late.
d Sorry. I can't get the phone because my hands are dirty.
e Do you know what you're getting for your birthday?
f I quite like Andrew, but I'm getting very annoyed at his rude comments.
g Helen got some fantastic new shoes in town today.

(96) I can … Tell the story of how I met a new friend

1 b I needed to get away. c My plane took off.
d I checked into an amazing hotel. e I filled in some forms.
f We bumped into each other. g I asked her out.
h We went out every night. i I found out that she already had a boyfriend. j I checked out of the hotel.

2 b off c up d out e off f into g out h in

(97) I can … Say that I feel the same as someone else

1 b 1 c 8 d 7 e 6 f 2 g 5 h 4

2 b So was I. c So did I. d So did I. e Neither did I.
f So have I. g Neither am I. h Neither do I.

(98) I can understand young people's colloquial conversations

1 b Kylie ~~was like~~ **asked**, 'What's your problem?'
c 'I ~~so~~ **really** don't like this music.'
d The teacher ~~goes~~ **asked**, 'What ~~you gonna~~ **are you going to** do about this bad homework?'
e She ~~was like~~ **asked**, '~~You wanna~~ **Do you want to** go into town?' and I ~~was like~~ **replied**, '~~Whatever~~ **Yes, if you like**'.

2 Students' own answers

Index